Engraved by Capewell & Kimmel from an Ambro. by Bogardus.

Yours ever affectionate
Eugenio Kincaid

THE

HERO MISSIONARY,

OR,

A History of the Labors

OF THE

REV. EUGENIO KINCAID.

BY ALFRED S. PATTON,

AUTHOR OF "LIGHT IN THE VALLEY," "MY JOY AND CROWN," ETC., ETC.

"The brother whose praise is in the gospel throughout all the churches."
2 Cor. viii. 18.

"We live in deeds, not years ; in thoughts, not breaths ;
In feelings, not in figures on a dial.
We should count time by heart-throbs. He most lives
Who thinks most, feels the noblest, acts the best."

New-York:
H. DAYTON, 107 NASSAU STREET;
INDIANAPOLIS, IND. : DAYTON & ASHER.
1858.

J. J. REED,
PRINTER & STEREOTYPER,
43 Centre-St., N. Y.

To the

REV. JOSEPH H. KENNARD, D.D.

AND

WILSON JEWELL, M.D.,

THE EARLY AND DEVOTED FRIENDS

OF

HIM WHOSE LABORS, IN PART, ARE HEREIN SKETCHED,

This Volume

IS AFFECTIONATELY AND GRATEFULLY INSCRIBED

BY

THE AUTHOR.

PREFACE.

On the day that Mr. Kincaid last left America to return to Burmah, I ventured to request permission to acquaint myself with all the accessible facts of his public life, with the view of giving them to the world in the shape of a book. The application was unexpected, but after some hesitation, it was modestly waved by referring the proposal to the two "early and devoted friends" whose names adorn a previous page. Having received their kind approval of such an undertaking, I began at once the preparation of this volume.

As expressed in the title, it does not claim to be a life of Mr. Kincaid, but a history of his labors, and these I have endeavored to sketch in a style adapted to the popular mind, and calculated, it is confidently hoped, to awaken increasing interest in the great enterprise to which all his energies have been given.

The simple design of this work, then, is to furnish a condensed, yet accurate view of the incidents and scenes connected with those bold and persevering efforts which mark Mr. Kincaid as "The Hero Missionary," and which have contributed to give him such eminence and honor among that noble band who have sought, or are now seeking, the evangelization of Burmah.

Carlyle, in his Life of Sterling, has said—"I have remarked that a true delineation of the smallest man and his scene of pilgrimage through life, is capable of interesting the greatest man; that all men are to an unspeakable degree brothers, each man's life a strange emblem of every man's; and that Human Portraits, faithfully drawn, are of all pictures the welcomest on human walls."

If this be true, then, surely the sketch of a man whose achievements in the highest sphere of human effort, have made him distinguished among his fellows, must be capable of awakening a still deeper interest, and a faithful portrait of such an one cannot fail to prove a most welcome addition to those already in the world's possession. But, beyond this, the hope is cherished that what is here recorded may serve to excite a deeper interest in the subject of Christian Missions, and thus contribute, in some humble measure, to advance a cause dear to all who possess the mind "which was also in Christ Jesus."

CONTENTS.

CHAPTER I.

PAGE

LIFE'S BEGINNINGS, - - - - - - - - - 11

CHAPTER II

ELEMENTS OF CHARACTER, - - - - - - - 23

CHAPTER III.

THE FOREIGN MISSIONARY, - - - - - - 33

CHAPTER IV.

ENTERING THE FOREIGN FIELD, - - - - - 41

CHAPTER V.

A YEAR IN RANGOON, - - - - - - - - 52

CHAPTER VI.

UP THE IRRAWADDY, - - - - - - - - 60

CHAPTER VII.

OPPOSITION AT AVA, - - - - - - - - 68

CHAPTER VIII.

THE GOSPEL IN THE GOLDEN CITY, - - - - 80

CHAPTER IX.

IN THE SHADOW OF THE HIMMALEH MOUNTAINS, - - - 89

CHAPTER X.

IN PERILS AMONG ROBBERS, - - - - - 103

CHAPTER XI.

DANGER AND DELIVERANCE, - - - - - - 116

CHAPTER XII.

LABORS IN TENNASSERIM, - - - - - - 129

CHAPTER XIII.

A GREAT WORK IN ARRACAN, - - - - - - - 145

CHAPTER XIV.

VISIT TO THE MOUNTAIN CHIEF, - - - - - - 159

CHAPTER XV.

VISIT TO AMERICA, - - - - - - - - - 177

CHAPTER XVI.

REOPENING OF BURMAH, - - - - - - - 195

CHAPTER XVII.

OFF AGAIN FOR BURMAH, - - - - - - - - 210

CHAPTER XVIII.

RESUMING LABORS, - - - - - - - 224

CHAPTER XIX.

HAVING FAVOR WITH THE PEOPLE, - - - - - 235

CHAPTER XX.

LABORS INTERRUPTED BY WAR, - - - - - - 245

CHAPTER XXI.

SETTING UP THE STANDARD AT PROME, - - - - 257

CHAPTER XXII.

IN FAVOR WITH THE KING, - - - - - - - 264

CHAPTER XXIII.

ON THE KING'S BUSINESS, - - - - - - - - 276

CHAPTER XXIV.

THE OVERLAND ROUTE TO BURMAH, - - - - - 285

CHAPTER XXV.

RETROSPECT AND PROSPECT, - - - - - - - 307

KINCAID—THE HERO MISSIONARY.

CHAPTER I.

LIFE'S BEGINNINGS.

"Before I formed thee I knew thee;—and I ordained thee a prophet unto the nations."—Jer. i. 5.

"As the sun,
Ere it is risen, sometimes paints its image
In the atmosphere; so often do the spirits of
Great events stride on before the events,
And in to-day already walks to-morrow."

The future of some men is clearly foreshadowed at life's beginning. Just as the naturalist in looking at the merest shoot discerns the pledge of a sturdy oak—so those who carefully observe the first developments of mind may foretell the probable future of the child. Alluding to the deep interest connected with such observations, Foster, in one of his Essays says—"While I anticipate the endless progress of life, and wonder through what unknown scenes it is to take its course, its past years lose that character of vanity which would seem to belong to a train of fleeting, perishing moments, and I see them assuming the dignity of a commencing eternity. In them I have *begun* to be that conscious existence which I *am* to be through endless duration; and I cannot be content without an accurate sketch of the windings thus far of a stream which is to bear me on for ever." A feeling of curiosity similar to this prompts us to inquire respecting the early history of others; and hence, when we hear of one who, in any of life's pursuits, has been successful in reaching a position of eminence and usefulness, we find ourselves almost instinctively asking for his antecedents.

Nor can we have failed to notice that, with few exceptions, whatever traits have been peculiar to one in the primary periods of his life, have contributed not a little to give shape and direction to his whole future existence.

But besides these mental and moral indexes, it is sometimes exceedingly interesting to notice the moulding influence of those *outward* circumstances which, though they may at the time appear trivial, nevertheless exert a power over an individual's inner history altogether disproportionate to their seeming importance.

A brief reference to a few such characteristics and circumstances connected with the youth and early manhood of EUGENIO KINCAID will occupy the limits of the present chapter. He was born in the little Connecticut town of WETHERSFIELD, but almost before the years of memory his parents removed to Canada, and finally settled in Pennsylvania.

His father, NOAH KINCAID, is a respectable physician, and still lives to rejoice in his son's usefulness. The maiden name of his mother (some years since deceased) was Lydia Hough. Both parents were consistent members of the Presbyterian church, and highly esteemed in the circle in which Providence allotted them to move.

EUGENIO was the oldest of eight children, and the pious instructions of his sainted mother—to whom he was peculiarly attached—are among his earliest and most cherished recollections. Almost from the day of his birth she seems to have had an impression that he would become more than an ordinary man, and, doubtless, the care and attention which this conviction prompted, had not a little to do in the development of his moral and mental powers, and consequently in giving direction to his whole future life.

His first years, though not marked by any striking display of genius, were yet distinguished by some intimations of peculiar talent; and any thoughtful observer would have seen in him that which gave a sure pledge of future eminence. While very steady, and devoted to study, he was at the same time remarkably energetic—exhibiting all that intense earnestness in whatever he undertook, that has characterized him through life.

At the age of sixteen, his mind became deeply exercised on the subject of religion. A meeting of days was at that time held by a traveling Baptist preacher, which he attended; and, before its close, he was brought by divine grace to exercise deep repentance for sin, and to experience a thorough change of heart. His mind was at once exercised in reference to the ordinance of Christian baptism, and going to the preacher he asked him for a book which might give him some light on the subject. The preacher went immediately to his saddle-bags, and, taking out a small volume, handed it to him. Upon opening it, Mr. Kincaid found it to be a New Testament, and, thinking he had made a mistake, immediately returned it—when the preacher, looking very earnestly at him, said—"Young man, if you want any better guide than the Holy Ghost has given, don't come to me." The remark was never forgotten, and, after a careful investigation of the subject, as presented in the word of God, he felt that there was no room to doubt, and at once with a willing mind, submitted to the ordinance. He was not brought to this decision, however, without a painful struggle, and in carrying it out he was obliged to encounter no small amount of opposition. Only a short time previous to this he had commenced the study of the law under the direction of his former pastor; but the day following his baptism he found that his books had been removed, and he was given to understand that he could no longer look to him for assistance.

Thus all his plans for the future seemed to be at once frustrated. He was not long, however, in suspense ; for God, who called him out of darkness into his marvellous light, had marked out another path for him, and he was soon made to feel it a duty to pursue a course of study with reference to the work of the ministry. At first, many difficulties beset his way, but, mastering these, he at length found his way to the Literary and Theological Institution at Hamilton, where he was graduated in 1822.

From the very day of his conversion he had been thoroughly imbued with the spirit of missions, and, during his preparatory studies, so deep were his impressions of duty to the heathen, that he resolved to devote his life to labors for their salvation. Upon the completion of his course at the Institution, therefore, he offered himself to the Baptist Board of Missions,—asking an appointment to Burmah. From various causes, however, but principally, it is believed, through the conservative counsels of one who regarded him as wanting in prudence, his application was declined, and his cherished hope was thus, for a time, deferred. Under these circumstances he was induced to accept an invitation to the pastoral charge of the Baptist church at Galway, N. Y. Here, in the midst of an attached people, it was his privilege for about three years to labor and to witness signal and most cheering success in his ministry. "His preaching," says one of the venerable men connected with that church, "was much to our satisfaction—he was greatly beloved by all, and we thought him a very promising young man." But happy as were all the circumstances connected with this settlement, he did not feel contented to remain there—wishing to labor in a more destitute part of the vineyard. In the year 1826 he made a visit of exploration into the valley of the Susquehanna, and finding there a wide and inviting field, he determined at once to enter it.

At this time there were not more than two or three Baptists in all that region ; and when, calling at the house of one of these, he introduced himself as a Baptist minister, the old man was quite overcome, and without making any reply, in an audible voice thanked God for this long-desired blessing.

Mr. Kincaid commenced preaching statedly at Milton, Union Co., and in less than six months a little church was organized in that town, consisting of nine members. The occasion of their first baptism is still remembered by many of the inhabitants of that place as an occasion of peculiar interest. It took place immediately upon the close of a Lord's day morning service, and was witnessed by a very large concourse of people. Public notice having been given that the ordinance would be administered on that day, it brought together not only the greater part of the floating population of that town and surrounding country, but the dispersing congregations of the other churches; and the river bank, thronged with this curious but attentive crowd, presented a scene at once impressive and beautiful. After baptizing two rejoicing converts, the pastor of the Presbyterian church, by request, closed the service with an appropriate and fervent prayer.

But, while making Milton his home, Mr. Kincaid embraced every opportunity of extending his labors into the surrounding towns and villages, and, among other localities, he was accustomed to preach occasionally at Warrior Run. His visits here had the effect of exciting an unusual interest, and a minister of another denomination, who regarded him in the light of an intruder, thought it important to warn his people against hearing "the young Baptist preacher," solemnly assuring them that "Baptist sentiments were the worst of all heresies; for when once they entered a place, they could never be rooted out." In addition to his numerous preaching engagements, Mr. Kincaid edited for a time THE LITERARY AND EVANGELICAL REGISTER, a monthly magazine, printed at Milton, and designed to diffuse general scientific and religious knowledge. From a variety of causes, however, its publication, after the first year, was discontinued.

Toward the close of 1828, the Board of the Baptist General Association of Pennsylvania, for Missionary Purposes,* selected Mr. Kincaid to preach the gospel, and to travel as an exploring agent in several of the central counties of the State. This appointment he accepted, and the cheering success which almost immediately crowned his efforts, is embodied in the following extracts from a letter, written under date of June 16, 1829, to the Rev. Mr. Kennard—

"After receiving an appointment as missionary and agent, I commenced my labors the first week in March. Without delay I traveled over the field in which I had labored for more than two years—the principal places are Milton, New Columbia, Sunbury, Shamokin, Washington, Jerseybower, Moreland, and Pennsborough. In most of these places, the prospect of good is encouraging; assemblies generally large and attentive. The discriminating doctrines of our faith begin to claim attention—a spirit of inquiry is going forth, and so far the result has been cheering. For some months past, Shamokin has been sharing in the special influences of the Spirit. The youth have shared largely in this work of grace. The number of anxious, mourning souls is increasing; and, what is worthy of remark, the largest number received their first conviction on baptismal occasions—some who

* An organization which, in 1838, was merged into the Pennsylvania Baptist State Convention.

came out of curiosity, others to ridicule, and others to blaspheme, were pricked in the heart, and began to inquire, 'what *shall* we do?' Some who were most violent opposers are *now* coming and offering themselves for baptism. The last two Sabbaths on which I baptised, seventeen were received into the church. On these occasions people flock together from all the surrounding country, and I have endeavored to explain faithfully the import of that commission which Christ gave to the Apostles.

Sunbury is an important place, and I think a church may be formed here soon—the Presbyterian meeting house is at our service when not in use.

Milton and the country around it is an interesting field of labor. I have been blessed in raising up a small church here, and several interesting young people have been added by baptism. This little church has commenced building a brick meeting house 34 by 40—they intend finishing it this summer. One baptised here a few days since; several inquiring souls.

I have visited settlements in this country where a sermon had never been preached. I have received letters from other neighborhoods, begging of me to come and preach to them. West of the Alleghany mountains is a vast tract of new country, stretching to the North and West, and settlements are forming in every direction. The inhabitants are generally intelligent and enterprising. I have seen, in this wilderness, females come ten and twelve miles on foot to hear one sermon. Many appear to be hungry for the bread of life. I have not traveled as yet any further than into Jefferson county—soon I intend to go over more ground. I feel anxious to know how much land we have to possess. *Pioneers* are needed to range through this new country and plant churches. The time has evidently *come* when the helping hand is to be put forth—every thing is encouraging ; it is a good cause, and the great Head of the church will prosper it. Difficulties there are, and opposition there will be ; but, who art thou, O great mountain? before Zerobabel thou shalt become a plain. Soon the wilderness will bud and blossom like the rose.—Let the gospel of Christ go forth, and it will not return void."

Mr. Kincaid continued in this service for several years, and, upon closing his connection with the Association, the Board, in their Annual Report, bore the following testimony to their appreciation of his labors—

"In concluding our report," says the secretary, "we wish to express our high sense of the valuable services rendered by our Brother Kincaid, in whose resignation, the Association sustains a great loss. He has been your agent from your first organization, and has been the chief instrument in originating nearly al' your auxiliary societies. As a pioneer, we know not his equal. It has been ascertained, that within the last four years, he has traveled more than 20,0 miles, in exploring our State, and preaching in its most destitute and dreary regions, and in some instances, where the feet of him that bringeth good tidings had never before been seen. We rejoice that the *Foreign Mission*, in which we feel a lively interest, has obtained a brother so laborious and self-denying."

The night before leaving Boston for India, Mr. Kincaid wrote the Board as follows :—

"The deep interest I have felt in the advancement of the cause in Pennsylvania, can never be erased from my mind; my happiness has been identified with the prosperity of the Mission cause in that State, and though I may never visit it again, the recollections of past years, will ever be present with me. In mind, I shall often visit those mountains and valleys where I have so frequently preached the things concerning the kingdom of God."

"So ardently," it is added, "was he devoted to the cause of missions in this State, and so unquestionable an assurance has he left of the sincerity of that devotion, as naturally to elicit from us warm expressions of gratitude. Indeed, it is difficult to suppress the inquisitiveness we feel in calling to recollection so worthy a friend—so devoted a Christian. We would fain know where he resides; the tenor of his life, and the success of his toils. Has he tired under his burden, and given up in despair? Or, is he pressing forward to victory and death, with unabated ardor?"

After detaining the reader with a brief reference to the natural elements of the man, whose life was so auspiciously begun, a full and satisfactory answer to these questions will be found, it is believed, in the succeeding chapters of this work.

CHAPTER II.

ELEMENTS OF CHARACTER.

"EVERY work that he began . . . he did it with all his heart and prospered."
2 Chron. xxxi. 21.

"He lives and breathes
For noble purposes of mind; and his heart
Beats to heroic things of ancient days;
His eye distinguishes; his soul creates."

MANY men seem to have no *individuality.* Even though enjoying what is called a *reputation,* they are wholly wanting in what constitutes a distinctive *character.* Neither their mental nor their moral attributes are marked by any thing that can be regarded as permanent, and but for a certain "vain show" they would pass through life scarcely challenging recognition. There are others, however, endowed with such gifts that it matters not where they may be placed, their presence and influence are sure to be deeply and widely felt. Nor is it difficult to discern the qualities which generally give to individuals position and power. In all such cases it will be found that the constituent elements of the mind are such as to impart a decided character to all they say and do, and by the confidence with which they speak their sentiments, and the boldness with which they execute their plans, they speedily establish a title to preëminence even among illustrious associates.

These natural traits have been strikingly exhibited in the life and labors of Mr. Kincaid, and to their possession must be traced one of the chief causes of his astonishing success.

To exhibit these traits is a difficult task, and one which I approach with great diffidence. In referring to a character so marked by Christian and manly virtue, however, nothing, of course, will be expected beyond a brief outline of the chief qualities for which he has become so widely distinguished.

The *intellectual* endowments of Mr. Kincaid, though not of the first or highest order, are unquestionably far above mediocrity, and the depth and breadth of their development, under the circumstances in which he has been placed, afford ample proof of their native scope and vigor. With a mind at once contemplative and discriminating, he exhibits also sleepless intellectual vivacity, and all his mental processes are conducted with the greatest possible rapidity. Hence it is that, notwithstanding the amount of time given to active labors, he has still been astonishingly successful in the acquisition of general intelligence.

Besides being an educated man, therefore, within his appropriate sphere, few, perhaps, are more familiar than he with the current history of the world, whether in the department of politics, science or religion. He possesses also remarkable resources in himself—in his good sense, his quick sagacity, his generous sensibilities, and his fertile imagination. Under no circumstances, perhaps, have these powers appeared to greater advantage than on the platform, when under the excitement induced by a crowded audience, he has been portraying the thrilling scenes connected with his labors in Burmah, or when, with strong argument and melting pathos, he has been heard pleading with the churches in behalf of the perishing heathen.

At such times, a whole assembly has been not only bathed in tears, but so thrilled by his graphic sketches, or so overwhelmed by his impetuous appeals, that the feelings of many have found utterance in involuntary, half-suppressed ejaculations.

The *physical* organization of Mr. Kincaid is scarcely less remarkable than his mental developments, and has doubtless contributed not a little to the making up of all the other elements of his manhood.

In person he is about the medium height, firmly, though not stoutly built—presenting a remarkable combination of nervous and muscular energy. As the natural result of such a formation, constituting the basis of an active temperament, he has, on all occasions, exhibited great powers of endurance, and evidently with a constitution less vigorous, he could never have survived the toils and privations through which he has been called to pass. The action of strong character, it has been said, demands something firm in its natural basis, just as massive engines require, for their weight and for their working, to be fixed on a solid foundation. The physical nature thus becomes an ally of the moral one, and with a hardness that never shrinks, sustains the energy that never remits.

This constitutional firmness may at least be regarded as an essental condition to *physical courage.* And among the many qualities requisite to the position of a Foreign Missionary, this certainly, is one of no little importance. In the prosecution of his work he is often thrown amid circumstances where timidity and irresolution would be ruin, and he needs, therefore, in an eminent degree, the power to provide against trying emergencies, and the bravery to ward off the most threatening danger.

The possession of this quality, giving to a man as it does, the full use of his faculties for the prudent and prompt adaptation of means to ends, is one of the rarest and most important of human endowments. Indeed, without a measure of this courage an individual can scarcely hope to succeed in any important undertaking, because, as Foster has said—" In almost all plans of great enterprise, a man must systematically dismiss, at the entrance, every wish to stipulate with his destiny for safety. He voluntarily treads within the precincts of danger ; and though it be possible he may escape, he ought to be prepared with the fortitude of a self-devoted victim. This is the inevitable condition on which heroes, travelers, or missionaries among savage nations, and reformers on a grand scale must commence their career."

But this dauntless spirit which is demanded in entering upon a great and hazardous enterprise is not less essential to its successful prosecution. And here we discover one of the strongest elements perhaps in Mr. Kincaid's character ; for while quick in his perceptions, and prompt and bold in forming his plans, he is at the same time persevering and confident in their execution. In his case we have a remarkable illustration of a strenuous will accompanying the conclusions of thought, and constantly inciting the utmost efforts to give them a practical result. And it matters not how formidable the difficulties, or how persistent the opposition which would defeat his plans, so inflexible is the temper of his mind, and so indomitable his courage, that such circumstances only increase the intensity of his soul, and with a feeling bordering on impunity, he seems almost to make his way through impossibilities, and reaches, at last, the full execution of his purposes.

But closely allied with this trait of character is another, I allude to his *independence.* Let it cost what it may, he will be honest to the convictions of his own mind, and without stopping to consider what he might lose or what he might gain by any particular course of action, his single inquiry is, What is right ? And having satisfied his conscience on this point, without the slightest regard to man's frown or the hope of his favor, he will say and do whatever he conscientiously believes to be true and proper.

His rule has been to act, as far as possible, from convictions superior to his own passions ; and being governed by views of duty too deep and strong to yield to those influences which too often lead men to act in a way which their better judgments would forbid, his course, in some instances, may appear indiscreet—savoring, perchance, of harshness and arrogance.

Frankly independent in his opinions, however, and not without what would be called strong prejudices—no uncommon feature of powerful minds—Mr. Kincaid has not been the man to play the sycophant, nor, under any circumstances, to feign himself what he is not, and a more perfectly outspoken and transparent soul I have never known. In truth—

> "My love doth so approve him,
> That even his stubbornness, his checks, and frowns,
> Have grace and favor in them."

If anything has been needed to temper this independence and guard it against abuse, that element has existed in his remarkable *self-devotement.* His, in an eminent degree, has been the spirit of him who "pleased not himself," and who said—"My meat and my drink is to do the will of Him that sent me, and to finish His work." He has emphatically *given* himself to the work ; abjuring, from the very beginning, every thing that has not looked to its accomplishment.

Without repining, he has relinquished all else that was dear to him, and, in a spirit of true self-denial, has brought into captivity every passion of his soul to the obedience of Christ. And having made this full surrender of himself, he has been content to derive all his happiness in laboring with ceaseless toil for the glory of God and the salvation of men. His intention has been single, his way straightforward, and, keeping his end in view, he has pursued it without defection and without weariness. Hence, while his natural courage has supported him amid dangers, and while opposition and perils have not been able to disturb his self-reliance, this feeling of his soul, leading him to look to a higher object, has enabled him to say with the Apostle—"Neither count I my life dear unto myself, so that I might finish my course with joy, and the ministry which I have received of the Lord Jesus, to testify the Gospel of the grace of God." His life and spirit are fitly embodied in a noble strain of the poet, that reads as if it were written for him :

"I feel a secret impulse drive me on,
And my soul springs impatient for the fight,
'Tis not the heated spirit and warm blood
Of sanguine youth with which my bosom burns ;
And though I thirst for glory, 'tis not, witness, Heaven ;
'Tis not the sinful lust of fading fame,
The perishable praise of mortal man ;
His praise I covet whose applause is life."

But, after all, the source of his abundant labors as well as the secret of his great success, must be traced to his wonderful *faith.* Deeply convinced, as he is, of the verity of the Divine promises, and taking these as the basis of his efforts, he is actuated by no visionary conceits, but by that principle which has the marvelous power of making the future present ; the unseen visible ; and of investing its possessor with strength sufficient to overcome seeming impossibilities.

This is the gift of which the Apostle speaks in the eleventh of Hebrews, and through which holy men of olden time, subdued kingdoms, quenched the violence of fire, stopped the mouths of lions, and turned to flight the armies of the Aliens. "The man of faith," says a gifted writer, "is a decided character. The instinct of his reason is a strong will, from a strong motive. He answers the questions, What will you do ? what will you be ? and says, I will walk worthy of my vocation ; I will be a son of God. The Almighty allows and grants what such a mind wishes. A man without a determined final faith, an undoubting trust in the true God, is but as a dry leaf on the wings of the wind, carried about by impulses unresisted and unavoidable. As the leaf cannot take root, and it rests but to rot, so the faithless man has no living power in him to draw vigor and beauty from the elements. There is no settled hope without faith, and therefore, no going forth of the prophetic and realizing soul into the future eternal firmament of the heavens ; but fancy, instead, makes dreams of memory, and amuses or terrifies with phantoms uncertain as the dance of moonbeams on the sea. Such a mind has no supreme good, for the sake of which every other object is felt to be inferior and to be held in abeyance, to be enjoyed or endured, merely as it may serve as means to the attainment of the grand end—the unalienable possession of that good."*

Animated by this "precious faith," Mr. Kincaid presents us with a living exemplification of its strength

* "Man and His Motives," by Geo. Moore, M.D., member of the Royal College of Physicians, etc., etc.

as a governing spring of action. It was in obedience to its dictates that he, in the first instance, relinquished the delights of home, with all the advantages of polished society, to live and labor among the heathen, and, amid the many discouragements which have beset him in his work, a confidence in God has overbalanced all hindrances, and a firm reliance on his word has not only banished all distrust, but filled his soul with an unwavering and sublime assurance of success. It is this faith, undoubtedly, that has given him that boldness, courage, perseverance and zeal, which, besides obtaining for him "a good report" among his brethren, have been crowned with a higher honor, put upon him by the Great Head of the Church.

Such, in outline, are some of the prominent traits of the man whose remarkable labors are sketched in the succeeding chapters. And thus, while furnishing a character every way worthy of study and emulation, the record of his public career, it is believed, will serve to awaken in every Christian heart increased confidence in the ultimate success of the glorious work of missions.

CHAPTER III.

THE FOREIGN MISSIONARY.

"Go ye into all the world, and preach the Gospel to every creature."
Luke xvi: 15.

"Home, thy joys are passing lovely—
Joys no strangeer heart can tell:
Happy home, indeed I love thee;
Can I, can I say, "Farewell?"
Can I leave thee,
Far in heathen lands to dwell?

Yes, I hasten from you gladly—
From the scenes I love so well:
Far away ye billows bear me;
Lovely native land, farewell;
Pleased I leave thee,
Far in heathen lands to dwell."

THE field in which Mr. Kincaid had now for several years been toiling, and from which abundant harvests had been gathered, was still full of promise, and on every hand he saw the most cheering evidence of the Divine blessing on his labors. With all this, however, he felt that God was calling him to another sphere of effort. And in the familiar words of one, afterwards associated with him in Missionary labor, he was forced to say—

> "My soul is not at rest. There comes a strange
> And secret whisper to my spirit, like
> A dream of night, that tells me I am on
> Enchanted ground. Why live I here?
>
> * * * * * *
>
> The voice of my departed Lord—
> "Go teach all nations," from the eastern world,
> Comes on the night air, and awakes my ear,
> And I will go. I may no longer doubt
> To give up friends, and home, and idol hopes,
> And every tender tie that binds my heart
> To thee, my country!"*

For months this conviction of duty had been forcing itself upon his mind. The cry of the perishing fell on his ear in tones deep and earnest as the wants and woes of millions. But at last the purpose was formed. He knew that while many were perfectly satisfied to labor at home, there were but few who had any deep impression of obligation to the heathen; a feeling confident that another would soon be found to preach the Gospel in the valley of the Susquehanna, he resolved to spend his future life in publishing tidings of peace to the benighted inhabitants of Burmah.

The one grand motive which impelled him to this decision was a zeal for the divine glory; and his duty was made clear by a deep conviction that the voice of

* Rev. N. Brown, D.D.

God was calling him to the work. There are many who would fain ascribe lower impulses to those who give themselves to such self-denying labors. And that a lower motive than the approbation of God may influence some who enter upon this work, we do not deny. "The circumstances," says Robert Hall, "which contribute to such a resolution are various, often too subtle and complicated to admit of a distinct analysis: a constitutional ardor of mind, a natural neglect of difficulties and dangers, an impatience of being confined within the trammels of ordinary duties, together with many accidental associations and impressions, may combine to form a missionary spirit." It is true, the very peculiarities of temperament and mind here referred to were strikingly characteristic of Mr. Kincaid. But, so far as can be discovered, no such circumstances contributed in his case to the decision of this momentous question, and his course having been marked out under a clear conviction of duty, he felt himself impelled to its discharge by all the impulses of a heart beating with love to God, and overflowing with sympathy for man.

Similar to these were the feelings of his companion, and to nothing could they mutually look forward with such deep anxiety and intense desire as the privilege of engaging in missionary labors among the heathen. At length the way was opened for the realization of their hopes, and Mr. Kincaid, as also

Mr. Mason, having been approved and accepted by the Baptist Board of Foreign Missions, were publicly set apart to the responsible office, on the evening of the 23d of May, 1830. The services connected with their designation were held in the spacious meeting-house of the Baldwin Place Church, in the presence, says a published report, of "an immensely crowded audience." On that occasion Mr. Kincaid delivered a discourse from 2 Cor. xiii, 11: "Finally, brethren, farewell. Be perfect, be of good comfort, be of one mind, live in peace; and the God of love and peace shall be with you." It was an affectionate valedictory, indicating a mind tenderly alive to the best interests of men; and giving proof that while he looked with earnest desire to benefit distant nations, he cherished a deep solicitude for the spiritual welfare of those from whom he was soon to be separated. At the close of the sermon, Dr. Bolles, in behalf of the Board, delivered an impressive charge, alluding in appropriate terms to the extensive field of their labor, the difficulties to be encountered, the zeal requisite to the work, the self-denial which the service demanded, and the pleasing encouragements presented of ample reward here, and of an eternal reward hereafter, as the result of their toils. Then with the aspect and style of fraternal and Christian affection, for which he was so remarkable, the Rev. Mr. Knowles presented to them the hand of fellow ship, accompanying the act with cheering words and pledging to them the fervent prayers of the churches for their safety and ultimate success.

On the following morning at 5 o'clock, just previous to the time of sailing, a prayer-meeting was held at the First Baptist meeting-house, where a large assembly met to unite in seeking the presence and blessing of the Lord to accompany his servants across the bosom of the deep and in the land of the heathen. At the close of this meeting, sorrowing, yet rejoicing, Mr. Kincaid took a final and affectionate leave of his brethren, adverting briefly to the deep sensibility which parting with Christian friends excited, but declaring that he felt unspeakably happy in prospect of so soon entering upon labors connected with the diffusion of the knowledge of the Saviour, among those who were sitting in the region and shadow of death.

Mrs. Kincaid, also, in tender accents, desired permission to present a parting word. Having for many years sighed for the opportunity of imparting instruction to Burman females, she was now made to rejoice at the prospect of a speedy consummation of her solicitous hopes and prayers, and for herself as well as in behalf of Mrs. Mason, she professed a readiness heartily to coöperate with their husbands in missionary labors.

After prayer, by the Rev. Mr. Choules, the assembly, with the missionaries, repaired to the ship, and. on the wharf, united in singing—

Ye Messengers of Christ,
His sov'reign voice obey;
Arise! and follow where he leads,
And peace attend your way

The Master whom you serve
Will needful strength bestow;
Depending on his promis'd aid,
With sacred courage go.

Mountains shall sink to plains,
And hell in vain oppose;
The cause is God's, and must prevail,
In spite of all his foes.

Go, spread a Saviour's fame:
And tell his matchless grace,
To the most guilty and deprav'd
Of Adam's num'rous race.

We wish you in his name,
The most divine success;
Assur'd that he who sends you forth
Will your endeavors bless.

Dr. Bolles, the Corresponding Secretary, then led in devout supplication to heaven for a prosperous voyage—that the winds and the waves might be propitious, and the seamen participate in the blessings of the Gospel, after which mutual salutations were exchanged, and the missionaries embarked on board the Martha, Capt. Lovett, for Calcutta.

As the vessel left its moorings, a solemn stillness

prevailed among the crowd of spectators, broken only by the smothered sobs of those who wept over the separation, and every heart sent up a silent, earnest prayer to that gracious and almighty Being, who holds the winds in his fist, and the ocean in the hollow of his hand, that he would not only waft them safely over the deep, but give them an open and effectual door among the heathen, and crown, with abundant success, all their efforts to shed over Burmah the saving light of truth.

Soon the vessel began to fade in the distance, and when straining eyes could no longer recognize the features of those on board, slowly they left the dock and returned to their several homes.

What the feelings of the departing missionaries were, may easily be imagined, though they have never been written. The ship was soon plunging her bows into the white crested billows, and when the last dim outline of their native land disappeared from view, Oh! with what sadness of heart did they retire to their lonely cabin! Now, as never before, they began to realize their situation. They had renounced the comforts and privileges of a refined and Christian land, henceforth to dwell among rude heathen. Every tender tie known to earth had been sundered, and having parted with fond parents, with loved brothers and sisters, and with happy circles of sympathizing Christian friends, they now felt, in all their intensity, the sundering of these endearing associations, and as they thought of them, their spirits well nigh sank within them.

It was under circumstances like these that Mrs. Judson made the following touching entry in her journal—"Still my heart bleeds. O, America! my native land; must I leave thee? Must I leave my parents, my sister and brother, my friends beloved, and all the scenes of my early youth; * * Where I learnt the endearments of friendship and tasted of all the happiness this world can afford; where I learnt also to value a Saviour's blood, and count all things but loss in comparison with the knowledge of Him! Yes, I must leave you all, for a heathen land, and an uncongenial clime. Farewell, happy, happy scenes—but never—no, never to be forgotten."

It was in that hour of trial and conflict with nature, that the missionary band, bowing together in prayer, looked alone to God for strength and were comforted.

"They prayed—they wept; but oh, how impotent
Is language to portray a scene like this!
No heart which has not felt its power, can know;
But, sure, if fervent prayer, meekly submissive,
Much avails with God, *that* prayer was heard in heaven'

CHAPTER IV.

ENTERING THE FOREIGN FIELD.

"Lo, I am with you always, even unto the end of the world."—Mat. xxviii. 20.

"Henceforth, then,
It matters not, if storm or sunshine be
My earthly lot—bitter or sweet my cup;
I only pray—God fit me for the work,
God make me holy, and my spirit nerve
For the stern hour of strife. Let me but know
There is an arm unseen that holds me up,
An eye that kindly watches all my path,
Till I my weary pilgrimage have done—
Let me but know I have a friend that waits
To welcome me to glory—and I joy
To tread the dark and death-fraught wilderness."

HAVING been borne in safety across the ocean, Mr. Kincaid reached Calcutta, Sept. 30, 1830, and from thence embarked for Maulmain, arriving there early on Lord's day morning, Nov. 28th. The exercises of his mind, awakened by the first view of the scenes among which he was henceforth to labor, are well expressed in the following extracts from a letter to the Rev. Dr. Bolles—"We gazed upon the scenery around us with feelings not easily to be described. The sun was just throwing his last rays on the distant hills—the country of Burmah lay before us, its mountains, its valleys, its rivers, and its numerous population. It was then we thought more feelingly than ever of the moral gloom that cast its deadly shade over all this portion of the globe ; it was then we felt more than ever for the missionaries who had toiled and suffered on these shores. * * How cheering is it to think of the change that will soon take place in Burmah! *Here* the Messiah will *reign*—paganism will give way before him, and all the proud ensigns of heathen superstition will crumble beneath his feet. All the Saviour has spoken, he will accomplish. This cheers the heart in this great moral desert."

A teacher having been employed, Mr. Kincaid commenced, at once, the acquisition of the language, but, while thus preparing himself to address the heathen, he was engaged also in preaching on the Lord's day, as well as on every Friday evening in English. Those who attended these services were chiefly British soldiers of the forty-fifth regiment, and Capt. Moore and other officers, observing the unusual attention paid to their interests, generously and promptly provided for their accommodation a new and commodious house of worship. On the assemblies convened in this chapel, God, in a signal manner, poured out his Spirit; converts were multiplied, and the church, before feeble, now became active and strong.

Mr. Kincaid, toward the close of the first year, spent in Maulmain, alluding to this work of grace, wrote as follows:—"Many a giant that defied the armies of the living God has fallen; not to perish, but to be raised to life everlasting. From about the middle of July to near the end of October, we have had a constant ingathering to the fold of Christ. It has been truly a time of refreshing from the presence of the Lord. Many who came out to the chapel to scoff, went home agonizing under the awakening influence of the holy Spirit."

As the result of this precious revival, about one hundred cases of conversion were reported, all of whom, after baptism, were added to the church. During the month of March, Mr. Kincaid, in company with Mr. Wade, made a tour of two or three hundred miles up the Martiban river to visit the Karens, who resided there in great numbers, and baptized nine persons on a profession of their faith in Christ. Returning from this excursion, Mr. Kincaid wrote—

"During our absence we have seen much of the goodness of our heavenly Father, and have had increasing evidence that the Lord has much people in idolatrous Burmah, to be called out of darkness into the glorious light of the gospel. Surely the *fields* are white for the harvest, and the urgency of preaching the gospel to the heathen gathers additional force at every step we take. Can any thing be more delightful, and more encouraging, than to see poor blind heathen at once transformed into the *image of Him*, who gave his *life* for sinners.

The Karens are a truly interesting people. But too little is known of their history, to say any thing about their origin, or the extent of their population; yet all agree in considering them very numerous in all parts of the Burman empire.

They are more mild in their manners, and more industrious in their habits than the Burmans; and although they are without any fixed religious principles, yet they are exceedingly superstitious. They attribute every evil they experience to the Nats, whom they propitiate by offerings and sacrifices of various kinds. They are entirely ignorant of the use of medicine; but for some reason they supposed we possessed skill superior to the influence of the Nats; for wherever we went, they brought their sick around us, and they were delighted and astonished at the salutary influence which our medicines produced."

In the midst of these encouragements, however, God was pleased to call his servant to the endurance of severe affliction in the sickness and death of a dear babe, and, also, of his beloved companion.

Mrs. Kincaid, who had been actively engaged in the study of the language and in the management of a school, heartily sympathized with her husband in all his labors and hopes. But, after suffering from several attacks of diseases peculiar to the climate, her strength was so much reduced as to preclude all hope of recovery. On the 10th of November, she was made the happy mother of a son, who, on the 8th of the following month, was removed by death. Just eleven days subsequent to this, her own career was terminated and her emancipated spirit took its flight to glory. The effect of these strokes on Mr. Kincaid is touchingly exhibited in the following extracts from a letter, addressed about this time, to a dear friend in the State of New York :—

"It becomes my painful duty to give a detailed account of some of the most afflicting events of my whole life. Hitherto I have been a stranger to sorrow—the cup of affliction has been dealt out to me with a sparing hand. My family was dearer to me than my own life, and a residence on this side the waste of waters, far from kindred and friends, serve to endear them a hundred fold. Separated as we were from the land of our fathers, and surrounded by thousands of poor ignorant heathen, our own humble home became a world of itself;—together we wept and prayed around the family altar, and together labored for the acquisition of that language, by which we might communicate the glorious gospel to the millions of Burmah. We entered into the work with the most sanguine hopes of ultimate success.

But now, sir, I am left to make my way alone on these pagan shores. The friend, the companion, the wife of my youth has been early called from the scene of her labors;—her toils are ended;—she weeps and prays no more. You know what it is to see the cold sweat of death gathering over affection's fairest form, and all that was lovely in life, fading and withering under the influence of deadly disease! You know what it is to shed tears of unavailing sorrow over the grave that encloses *one* dearer than life! After we arrived in India, we were blessed with excellent health, until the rainy season began; then we had a slight attack of intermittent fever, but after about ten days it left me, without taking a single portion of medicine;—it was otherwise, however, with Mrs. Kincaid. She had this fever at intervals for about two months, but it seemed to wear upon her but very little, so that she continued studying the Burman language. At this time she had an attack of the bowel complaint, which reduced her very fast. Both the fever and the bowel complaint were soon removed, but their debilitating influence had been the means of bringing on another disease, peculiar to this climate, and very fatal to foreigners. Until this time we had apprehended nothing alarming. Dr. Brower, of the 45th Regiment, attended daily, and Dr. Anderson, of the staff, often attended in council. These gentlemen advised, as the only effectual remedy for this complaint, a removal to some northern climate, as soon as Mrs. K. should be able to go on board ship. On the 10th of November, Mrs. Kincaid was made the happy mother of a son. Herself and child during the first five days were very well, and we had every prospect of getting out to sea in a short time.

On the 10th she was taken worse, so much so, that I relinquished all hope of her recovery; however, about the 28th and 29th every symptom appeared favorable. She expressed an anxiety to get out, thinking that a little change would prove serviceable both to body and mind. The physicians approved of it, and I had her carried out in a palanquin, morning and evening, until the 5th of December. Our little babe was taken ill on the 5th, and continued sinking until the 8th, when it went into convulsive fits; from the first fit he recovered, but a few hours after, he went into the second, and expired. Mrs. Kincaid sat in a chair, and held him in the last fit. I begged of her for my sake, and for hers not to exert herself; but a mother's affection prevailed over her better judgment. However, when she saw that its emancipated spirit had taken its upward flight, she became entirely calm, and felt so well satisfied that it was all for the best, that she often told me, she had not had one wish to have her sweet babe restored to her again. We both felt that this entire resignation to the will of God, was a kind mercy of our heavenly Father. From this time to the 15th of December, there was no perceptible change, except a gradual loss of strength. Most of the time previous to this date, I had felt an awful presentiment on my mind that my dear wife would not recover; but any favorable change filled me with hope.

The first of November, I laid aside my books, and relinquished all labors except to preach to the English, and made it my whole business, night and day, to administer to her wants. December 18th, Lord's day, I perceived that the disease was rapidly approaching a fatal crisis. After considerable conversation, I told her it was time for meeting, and that I had one person to baptize. She said—'Very well, but you will return as soon as pos-sible.' I returned before twelve o'clock, and we had as much conversation as her strength would permit. After preaching again in the evening, on this subject, 'For our light afflictions which are but for a moment,' &c., we both felt that this probably would be the last evening we should spend together on earth. I told her this separation to me was awfully painful, but I perceived it to be the will of God. She said her hope was in Christ, but she had not that cheering prospect which she wished, yet she felt weaned from the world, and could leave her family in the hands of

God. Much to the same purpose was said at intervals till eleven in the evening, when she urged me to lie down a little time and rest, (perceiving that I was much exhausted). At one o'clock I got up, and seeing that she was fast going, I gave her some lavender, which revived her, and she fell into an easy sleep till about two, when she awoke and said to me with a clear voice, 'I am now dying,' and, raising her eyes, continued silent. I applied some restoratives to her temples, but soon perceived the cold clammy sweat of death gathering on her forehead. After a little time, a heavenly smile came over her countenance, and more of the divine presence I never felt; —there was something friendly in the approach of death, and with pleasure I could have unrobed myself and descended with my dear companion into the dark valley:—heaven seemed to be just at hand, and the glories of the eternal world rose in delightful and awful majesty before me. Never before did I feel such strength in prayer. Never before such entire resignation to the will of God. I stood in silent watchful attention to see the spirit fling its last look on the world, and wing its way to the throne of God. After this she did not speak, but continued looking upwards, with a countenance that indicated that she had caught a glimpse of the brighter visions of eternity. About four o'clock on the morning of December 19th, she resigned up her spirit, without a struggle or a groan. When I saw that all was over, I called a Burman female, who was sleeping in an adjoining room, and said to her in the Burman language, 'The teacheress is dead.' The sound awoke little Wade, and springing from his bed, he cried out in the most heart-rending manner, 'Is my ma dead? Is my ma dead?' and for a time he was inconsolable. Few children of his age ever received more instruction from a parent. During the last six or eight months his dear ma labored much to instruct him in the knowledge of religion, and often took him alone, and prayed for him. Impressions were made on his mind which I trust will never be forgotten.

Thus, my dear sir, I have given you a hasty narration of facts, and you know how to sympathize with me. God has prepared me beyond any thing I had expected, to endure this trial. I see that God has done it, and I feel no disposition to murmur. Every effort was made which kind and skilful physicians could make to arrest the progress of the disease, but all proved unavailing; and I can now see that my dear Almy had been preparing to leave the world. At times she felt much distress of mind, and very often talked of the hardness of her heart; at other times she felt comforted with the promises of the gospel, and rejoiced in the hope of immortality.

Some of the most lovely and amiable dispositions which adorn the people of God, she exemplified in her life. That meekness and humility which shrinks from observation, and feels its own unworthiness, and induces a person to esteem others as better than himself, she did possess in no ordinary degree. She is now gone to the full participation of that rest which remains for the people of God: the darkness, and hardness of heart over which she mourned, and so often wept, are now removed, and her spirit, all beauteous and holy, joins the society of the redeemed in the paradise of God. A little time longer we travel in this vale of tears, and then hasten to join our friends who have gone before us. The way is short —the time is near—and how amiable, how lovely is the Christian religion, when brought in close connection with the lowly couch of death! It is the hand that wipes away every tear; it is the balm that heals the wounded spirit; it is the eye that looks undaunted on the king of terrors; it is that friend that sticketh closer than a brother."

CHAPTER V.

A YEAR IN RANGOON.

"A light to lighten the Gentiles."—Luke ii. 32

"The heathen lands, that lie beneath
The shades of overspreading death,
Revive at His first dawning light,
And deserts blossom at the sight."

Early in the spring of 1832, Mr. Kincaid removed from Maulmain to Rangoon, and, though not yet able to preach in the Burman tongue, he was eminently successful in carrying on the schools which had previously been established, and, also, by the aid of native assistants, in maintaining many of the public services of the mission. His deep conviction, even at this time, however, was that preaching must be relied on as the chief instrumentality for the conversion of the heathen. "The circulation of the Scriptures," said he, in a letter to the Secretary, "awakens attention; and, in some few instances, souls may be saved without the use of any other means. But the history of the church in all past ages confirms me in the opinion, that we ought not to expect the demolition of the kingdom of darkness, and the building up of the Saviour's, only as we go forth in faith, preaching the word of eternal life." To the same point is his testimony, given at a later date and as the result of his observations in another field:

"The longer I continue among the heathen, the more I am convinced that the Gospel conveyed by the living voice, is the means appointed for the conversion of men. Reading of books enlightens, and induces a spirit of inquiry; but the full and overflowing heart reaches the conscience, and awakens the finer feelings of the soul. Hence the necessity of preaching the word, of being instant in season and out of season. Could we but feel as we ought, we should know how to estimate the claims of these millions, on whom not one gleam of moral light has dawned for ages. It is not enough that we pray for them; it is not enough that we give them books; we must preach Jesus Christ, and not be discouraged amidst reproaches and insults."

At the close of the year, Mr. Kincaid went to Madras, where he was married to Miss Barbara McBain, daughter of a military officer in the service of the East India Company. During his absence those whom he had left in charge of the schools and of the general interests of the mission, were seized by an inferior officer of the government, and subjected to such fines and cruel punishments as had the effect of breaking up the schools, and of intimidating many who, under other circumstances, would have resorted for conversation and instruction to the Zayat.

On his return to Rangoon, however, notwithstanding these unfavorable occurrences, Mr. Kincaid boldly resumed his labors, and was soon visited by great numbers, not only from the city, but from distant provinces. This was especially the case during the famous annual festival of Gaudama, and, though many came to inquire about the truths of science, or the operations of the printing press, yet not a few seemed serious and anxious to gain a knowledge of the new religion.

Others, however, came as disputants. Thus, in one instance, while discoursing from his veranda, a Burman teacher, interrupting him, inquired—

"'Is God without *beginning* or *end*, and is he exempt from *old age* and *death?*'

'It is true.'

'And where is God?'

'In heaven.'

'Has God a body?'

'He is a spirit.'

'How shall we know this, when we cannot see him?'

'Just as you know you have a soul, though you cannot see the soul with the eyes of the body.'

'After death, will we see God?'

'Before death, if you receive divine light.'

'What is it?'

I then read to him, as the multitude gathered around us, several passages about Christ, his coming into the world, his death on the cross, and his resurrection. To believe in Christ, to repent of your sins, and pray for the Holy Ghost, is the way to receive divine light, and to have great peace of mind, and to be free from darkness, and from the fear of death."

At another time a government man entered while he was discoursing to about thirty or forty from the veranda, and in a vehement manner began to prove, in his own estimation, that all religions were the same.

He went on for about half an hour, rose suddenly and walked away. The assembly gazed so intently on Mr. Kincaid, that he was conscious they expected some reply. He therefore said to them—"*That man* has many words, but they give no light. You all know there is true silver, and there is false silver; there are false gods, and a true God. If there is a false god there is a false law; and if there is a true God, there is a true law. A man who has a little light will consider this, and desire to know the true God." Several at once exclaimed—"This, Sir, is true."

Among those who presented themselves about this time as inquirers, were many cases of peculiar interest.

On one occasion, returning from a walk, he found in the house a young man, a relative of the governor's wife, who for several days had been an attentive listener to the instructions imparted from the veranda. Shortly after this he came to the house, just at sun-rise, to engage in conversation and prayer, and, after breakfast, he came again to join in worship. "I see and feel too much," he said, "ever to abandon the cause of Christ."

At another time, when present at evening worship—he appeared quite affected, and two or three times, in the midst of the sermon, he said aloud, "*This is wonderful!*"

Subsequently he called very frequently, though generally after dark, giving on each visit convincing proof of growth both in knowledge and grace.

About the same time, a man called who lived two hundred miles beyond Ava; he was past the middle age of life, very intelligent and talked like a Christian—a tract, he said, had fallen into his hands about twelve or fourteen months ago; he read it, and resolved to know more about it, and if possible, see the man who taught this religion. He said—"*A great light is visiting the world!*"

During the same month a government man called, saying, that ever since he first heard he had been anxious to hear again. Just as he was leaving, Mr. Kincaid said—"Where will you go when you die?—Is it all dark?" He looked up with a countenance indicating a feeling not easily expressed, but made no reply. Mr. Kincaid then said—"The calamity of death terrifies you; God you reject, idols you worship, and you are ripe in years; what is beyond death?" The old man, shaking his head, replied—"*It is all dark.*"

Passing through the street one day, a young man came after him and inquired—

"Are you a teacher of religion?"

"Yes; what do you want?"

"A book," he replied, "that tells about God and Jesus Christ."

Moung Zoo-the, a young man of promising talents, and for some time an inquirer, having applied for baptism, Mr. Kincaid said to him—

"Are you not afraid to be baptized?"

"I have been, but it is gone now, and I feel strong."

"But suppose you are seized, put in prison, and beat with a bambo; will you be strong then?"

"I cannot deny Christ."

"But suppose they kill you?"

"Let them kill," he said, "I desire to follow Christ." Others, however, were not so bold. The fear of persecution operated in many cases to hinder a public profession of religion—so that at this very time, Ko A, one of the native assistants, reported that there were more than twenty in and about Rangoon who loved Jesus Christ, and were praying and serving God in secret.

Some who came from a distance said, "Why do you not go to Ava and all the great cities of the empire? Many have heard of the new religion and the books, and wish to understand what it is."

Favored with such indications of the divine blessing as these instances afforded, Mr. Kincaid, when asked by a Burmese officer of government how long he intended to stay, might well say—"UNTIL ALL BURMAH WORSHIPS THE ETERNAL GOD."

And we can easily imagine what faith and hope inspired his heart when he wrote,—

"The fields are really whitening for the harvest—the spirit of inquiry appears to be very extensive, and is daily becoming more so—the despotic nature of the government and the tyranny of the rulers lifts a most formidable obstacle to any change in the civil or religious establishments of the empire. But He who overturned the walls of Jericho, by means that mocked all human wisdom, is able to break down the strongholds of Satan here, and purify this land of all its abominations. The leaven is evidently at work—the most devoted Boodhists think that this religion will prevail. Satan, however, will make an effort, and his struggle may be long or short, according to the will of heaven. Let all who know Jesus Christ pray for the coming down of the Holy Spirit, that this wilderness may bloom like Eden."

CHAPTER VI.

UP THE IRRAWADDY.

"Blessed are ye that sow beside all waters."—Isa. xxxii. 20.

"Walk
Boldly and wisely in that light thou hast,
There is a hand above will help thee on."

On the 6th of April, 1833, Mr. Kincaid embarked on board a Burman boat for Ava. The journey up the Irrawaddy from Rangoon was seven hundred miles. He was accompanied by his wife and her sister, both English ladies, by Ko Shoon and Ko Sanlone, two native preachers, and by several other Burmans. At their departure Ko A, Moung Eu, and a number more of the disciples in Rangoon, accompanied them to the water, affectionately bidding them God-speed, and promising them a constant remembrance in prayer. Shortly after starting, their boat was found to have sprung aleak, and the water came in so rapidly as to require one man to keep bailing. Before night, however, they succeeded in discovering the leak, and, having stopped it, the next morning they proceeded on their way.

Among the chief dangers which beset them in this journey, was their constant exposure to attacks from robbers. Several times, indeed, they were in villages where robbery and murder had just been committed, and, in one instance, their escape seemed to be almost miraculous. While doubling a point in the river, a band of ten men rose upon them, all armed with spears, Burman swords, and one gun. At the same instant two boats made their appearance and came toward them with great rapidity. The men cried out, "Teacher, come quick; the robbers are upon us." The first company of ten men immediately fled on seeing the armed boats. Mr. Kincaid begged his boatmen to stay and help against the robbers, but all in vain; they fled, leaving only six beside himself, to face twenty-three men who were rushing rapidly towards them. They were ordered to stop again and again, but utterly refused. As the last resort, Mr. Kincaid called the men to follow him, and, rushing toward the approaching robbers, he threatened them if they did not stop instantly. Just at that moment a large Burman boat hove in sight, and came down the river; this, together with Mr. Kincaid's firmness, brought them to a stand. They turned about and made off rapidly in the same direction they had come. Thus were they mercifully preserved from the hands of unfeeling savages.

But these dangers were soon forgotten amid the

striking and cheering instances which they were so soon permitted to witness of the power and spread of the gospel. Almost every day was marked by some occurrence which served to strengthen faith in the ultimate triumph of the truth.

One man, for instance, came, saying that many months before, he had obtained a book in Rangoon, that told him about the eternal God, who made all things ; and about Christ, who died to open the way for the forgiveness of sin. He said " the more he had thought of this, the more it stuck to him that it was true."

In the city of *Thir-a-wan*, many said, " We want to hear more of this religion,—if it is true that there is a God who is free from sickness, old age and death, he must be the most excellent." Five men also declared their conviction of the truth, and determined to read and examine.

At a large village beyond this, while listening to the preaching, a woman cried out, " *This God is the true God ; this doctrine is the divine communication !*" Afterwards, in private conversation, she said, as soon as she heard, the truth shined upon her mind, and she saw instantly that, all her life, she had been stupidly worshiping what was no God.

While stopping at *Mey-an-oung*, the chief secretary of the city, though at first opposed to the distribution of the tracts and books, after hearing some passages read, said—"*These books teach the true God,*" and would not be satisfied until he had got one of every kind, nor would he let them go until a meal had been prepared and they had eaten.

Still further on they met with a government man, who said he had heard much about their books, and one of them he had heard read; ever since he had been anxious to get some of the books. He called all his men, told them to ask for books, and read about the eternal God. This man frankly admitted that he had long had doubts about Gaudama's religion, and these had been increased by hearing two or three great men in Ava declare their conviction that this new religion was true, and would spread through the country. He appeared to be very sincere, having a heart, disposed by the power of God, to receive the Gospel.

While at *Poung-day*, an ancient city about as large as Rangoon, Mr. Kincaid was invited to go to the house of the great Toung-diven teacher, so called, the head of the most powerful dissenting sect in Burmah. Arriving at the house, he found a venerable old man, and thirty or forty more, who had gathered to hear them talk. Upon asking him if he had ever read the word of God, he said—

"I read about a year ago, one small book that reasoned about the eternal God and Gaudama."

"What do you think?"

"I have remained careless."

"Then you are indifferent whether you are right or wrong; so there is no use of my saying any thing to you."

During the conversation, which lasted for some time, the old man said he was anxious to know why we took so much trouble to publish this religion. "For I see," said he, "that you are exposed to danger, and are very much reviled and reproached, and must be continually among strangers who do not care for you."

"Yes, and we are willing to suffer all this, and much more to save the Burmans from the punishment of hell."

The interest of the old teacher was so great that he afterwards followed Mr. Kincaid to the boat to hear more and obtain books.

The most thrilling incident, however, occurred at the town of *Tha-ret.* It is thus related by Mr. Kincaid:—

"While I was giving away some tracts to a crowd of people that lined the shore, a young man of an interesting appearance came near, and said, 'Will you please give me St. John's History of Christ, and the Acts of the Apostles?' 'Did you ever read these books?' 'Yes, teacher Judson gave them to me in Prome; but when the city was burned, I lost the books.' I gave him the books, and four tracts, and he immediately disappeared in the crowd. Soon after this we moved our boat one or two miles farther up the town, where we would be more secure from the wind. I could not help thinking of this young man, but did not expect to see him again. However, at dark he made his appearance, and said, there is a man in this city besides me who believes in Jesus Christ, and he wants to see the *teacher*, and get *books*, but he thinks the boat is away and has sent me to search. We followed the young man, and how were we surprised and almost overjoyed to find a venerable old man full of faith and hope in Christ, though he had no other teacher than St. John's History of Christ, and the View, accompanied by the influence of the Holy Spirit. He said he had loved Christ for about two years, and his language was that of a man who was acquainted with his own heart. He spoke distinctly of the carnal and spiritual mind, of regeneration and baptism. The young man before mentioned, had heard Dr. Judson preach in Prome, and had got books; afterwards he brought them to this town, and read them to this old man, and both I trust are born of God. I do not know when I have spent such an evening. To find two pilgrims in this great desert—to hear them speak so boldly and decidedly of their love to Christ in the presence of more than forty persons, filled me with joy. Surely this is the work of God! the power of the cross is felt in this dark land. O Burmah! Burmah! cast away thine idols, and hear the word of the Lord."

While laying before a town, a short distance below Ava, three or four hundred, as had often been the case at other places, gathered along the shore and listened to the words of eternal life. Among several cases of interest that here came to the knowledge of Mr. Kincaid, was one of a man about forty years of age. He said that some months before he had read a small book that made known to him the living God: at first he remained careless, but afterwards his mind shook, (as he expressed himself,) and he was afraid to worship idols any more; at the same time, he knew not how to worship the eternal God.

"Can you, sir," said he, "give me the divine communication?"

"Here, sir," said Mr. Kincaid, giving him all the Epistles, "are the words of the most high God; you must believe in Christ and pray for divine light."

The morning of the 20th of May brought them in sight of Ava. They had traveled fifty-four days, and had visited on their way about three hundred cities and villages. In most of these they had preached the Gospel, and in all of them had freely scattered books and tracts. Their Christian courage and faithfulness—their dangers and deliverances—the evidence of the spreading influence of Christianity—the awakened spirit of inquiry—the new fields of labor found ripening for the harvest—all conspired to make this excursion one of remarkable interest both to the brethren in Burmah and to the friends of missions in America.

And now, the journey finished, Mr. Kincaid looks upon what is to be the scene of his future labors. That there are difficulties and trials before him he knows, and that he is in himself inadequate to the achievement of his mission he deeply feels, "but," says he, "I enter this great city relying on the pledged promises of Him with whom is the residue of the Spirit:" and then, with intensest feeling he is heard to pray—"*O, Power Divine! shed abroad thy life-giving Spirit, that those who hear the Gospel may feel its power!*"

CHAPTER VII.

OPPOSITION AT AVA.

"No weapon that is formed against thee shall prosper; and every tongue that shall rise against thee in judgment thou shalt condemn. This is the heritage of the servants of the Lord."—Isaiah liv. 17.

"He'll shield you with a wall of fire,
With holy zeal your heart inspire,
Bid raging winds their fury cease,
And calm the savage breast to peace."

THE reception which Mr. Kincaid met with on his arrival at Ava, was very different from that which had cheered him in the villages and cities visited on the way. He was greatly perplexed in the first instance to find a house in which he could dwell with his family, even for the briefest period. After repeated delays, and when he had found it impossible to obtain a government order by which he might legally take up his abode in the city, he determined to take possession of a house without waiting for permission from the authorities, and through the efforts of Ko San-lone he, at length, succeeded in obtaining a house on the bank of the river to the east of the city. Only three days after taking possession of the house, however, the owner, an old lady of noble blood, died; and, having no children, the property fell into the hands of the king. By the royal favor, this house was transferred to one of the king's physicians, who immediately despatched a messenger ordering the premises to be at once vacated. The next day the royal doctor came himself. At first he talked loud, and behaved quite uncivil, threatening some Burmans who were listening to the gospel. At length he became calm, and, reasoning with him, Mr. Kincaid said, "This house is yours, but I cannot leave it until I obtain another; and another I cannot get without a government order. I am looking for a house, and expect an order soon." This seemed satisfactory. "Every day," writes Mr. Kincaid in his journal, "I called on a *Woon-gee* or *At-wen-woon*,* and, sometimes, on two or three in a day, asking for permission to rent a house, and always met with encouraging words. They had excuses for every delay and every broken promise. The young prince must have his ears bored. This took up eight or nine days. The Chinese ambassador was just taking his leave of the Burman court. This was an excuse for four or five days. Four wild elephants were to be caught. This took

* *Woon-gee*, this is the title of those composing the king's first council. *At-wen-woon*, this is the name given to the second council, each of these councils being composed of four members.

up three days. Thus it went on from day to day. One morning I called on Moung Sa, one of the *Woon-gees*, the same man who was an *At-wen-woon* when brother Judson first visited Ava. His countenance changed. What had taken place I could not tell. He had always appeared pleasant. I remained silent, waiting to hear the worst. The *Woon-gee* said—

'The king is pained to hear that, in Rangoon, and in all the cities and villages along the river, you have given books, and preached to the people. It is not agreeable to the king to have a new doctrine spread among his subjects. It is, therefore, the order of his majesty, that this English and American doctrine spread no further.'

'You know that I am a teacher of religion, and can I not preach to the people?'

'Yes, but you must not give books. Why do you not preach and give books to the Musselmen and Catholics?'

I told him I had come to Ava to preach to all people, of whatever nation; and if I am not allowed to go on I shall leave Ava, and go to some other nation. I could perceive in the course of this morning's conversation, that this nobleman had a rooted aversion to foreigners, or else that he felt it to be for his interest to appear so."

When the royal doctor parted from Mr. Kincaid he seemed willing to wait until another dwelling could be secured, but, on the following day, he sent his furniture, with an order to put it into the house. This they were forbid to do, and in a little time the doctor came with about twenty young men, to assist in carrying out the order. "I was sitting," says Mr. Kincaid, "in the door, and immediately began to reason with the doctor on the impropriety of using violence; that I was a stranger, in a strange land; that if our books and clothes were put into the street they would all be destroyed. The doctor was inexorable; cursed me, and all foreigners; reviled the Christian religion, and threatened my life. He then ordered his men to take his things in, and put me, my family, and all that belonged to us, into the street. Two young men in an instant rushed to the top of the stairs, to seize me. I pushed them down, and barred the door, so that from all their efforts, they could not force their way in.

Captain Low had got word of my situation, and sent me two letters in the forenoon, but the messengers were stopped and sent back. Two men were sent to Moung Sa, a *Woon-gee*, and he just said, 'What can I do?' Ouk-moo, whom I had sent away, was detained a prisoner in the street. About three o'clock, Ko San-lone returned, having been in search of a house. As soon as he entered the veranda, the doctor seized him, threw him down, and several of the young men fell upon him. This was too much to endure: his cries pierced my heart. I unbarred the door, and, with a cane in my hand, rushed out, threatening them. Instantly, they let go of him, and took up bamboos, pointed at one end, and Burman spears, and rushed upon me like young tigers. I knocked five of them over with my cane, but only one was injured. The door was again barred; and, for the first time, the doctor was disposed to reason. As soon as I perceived this, I threw open the door and told him to come in. He said he had been very angry, and behaved bad; and begged I would forget it.

The same evening, the British Resident learned from Captain Low nearly all the occurrences of the day. He wrote to the ministers thus, 'I am sorry to hear that a Burmese, named Oo-boy, has assaulted and threatened Mr. Kincaid and his family; and that no notice has been taken of it by the ministers, although one of the *Woon-gees* was sent to, when the affair began. In the most savage countries in the world, teachers of religion are treated with kindness and respect; and when the news of this affair shall reach Bengal, England, and America, the people will cry, Shame!' I had no knowledge of this till the 22d, when I received letters from the Resident and Captain Low, saying, 'I hope you will not by forgiveness save Oo-boy from merited punishment.' Before noon I was requested to appear at the *Loot-dau,* where all the ministers of state were assembled, with the queen's brother at their head. After hearing the whole affair from first to last, they said, 'We know you are right, and this man deserves punishment; but as he is the king's doctor, and as you are a teacher of religion, which enjoins forbearance and forgiveness, we hope you will forgive him, and he shall confess at any time and in any place you direct.' I said, you must understand that it was not I who brought up this subject, neither did I request it. However, so far as I am personally concerned, I cheerfully forgive the man; but he must confess his wrong in the presence of all the great ministers. They then said, 'Do you wish him to be put in prison, and whipped?' I said 'No; I only wish to secure myself and family from being insulted by rude and ignorant people. They further said, 'The fact that you forgive a man who has done so bad will be known all through the empire, and many will be inclined to examine your doctrine.'—Thus we parted—the *Woon-gees* at the same time giving me a written document which was a permission to rent any house I should choose. The British Resident hearing these things, was not satisfied, and dispatched another message, saying, 'As Mr. Kincaid is an American, he can do as he pleases; but as Mrs. Kincaid and her sister are British subjects, he was bound, as the representative of his Government, to see that those who should dare insult them, should receive merited punishment.' Furthermore, as Oo-boy had, openly in the streets of Ava, reviled the Christian religion, he considered his crime deserving severe punishment. At the same time he requested a boat, that the whole account of this affair might be sent, without delay, to Major Burney, in Rangoon. This alarmed them, and the doctor was put in prison. The Resident was still dissatisfied. He wrote again, complaining of the unwillingness of the ministers to punish him as his crimes deserved: said it was because he was the royal physician; but he urged this as an additional reason why he should not be spared. 'If,' said he, 'Oo-boy was a poor, ignorant man, there would be room for mercy; but a man of his rank deserves none.' Immediately Oo-boy was put in the stocks, and the Resident sends a man every day to see that he is not screened from justice. I feel very much for his wife and children—they visit us every day and beg that we would intercede for him. The doctor is continually sending to me, to make an effort in his favor. I would gladly restore him to his family, if it was in my power."

Shortly after this Mr. Kincaid succeeded in obtaining a house, west of the palace, and near the centre of the city. Here he was soon permitted to witness manifestations of the same eager spirit of inquiry which he had met with along the Irawaddy. "Inquiry," says he, writing to one of his missionary brethren, "is abroad, is spreading, and the smothered flame will burst ere long. Many government men call. Among these, two of the head writers call, read, and listen. Probably they are spies. I have always seen these men among the *Woon-gees*. Having begun to preach the gospel here, there is no going back. It is impossible to work in the dark, or work quietly, as some would call it. I am quite certain that I have not taken a step but a government man has been on my heels. It is well. I have adopted one course to pursue; that is, to preach Christ to every person, and leave the consequences to Him who has promised to give the heathen to His Son for an inheritance."

His impressions with reference to being under the jealous eye of officers of government soon proved to be well founded. One of the *Woon-gees* showed himself particularly hostile, and on no less than ten occasions positively forbid him preaching the gospel and giving books. On the 22d of March, 1834, a message came directing an immediate appearance before the high court of the empire. Upon presenting himself, one of the *Woon-gees* said sternly to Mr. Kincaid—

"Why have you come to the royal city?"

"To diffuse abroad the knowledge of the eternal God."

"Dare you say the religion of the king, his princes, his nobles, and his people, is false?"

"No, my lord, I do not say so; but in my own

country, and in all the world, before the knowledge of the living God appeared, the people worshiped idols, and the command of God is, to go into all the world, and preach this religion."

"Stop: it is not proper to say much. It is the wish of the king, his ministers, and myself, that you should preach no more."

"If you send us away, the whole world will ridicule you. Why, my lord, are you afraid of two men?"

"We do not wish you to remain here: you may go to Rangoon."

"Are there no other towns where we can go?"

"Rangoon is a good place; go there."

"Much conversation," says Mr. Kincaid, "took place about our disciples, our books, and various subjects connected with the propagation of religion. In my conversation, which lasted some time, I used respectful but firm language. I told him we had no political motive, no connection with any earthly power; that our only object was to teach the people the law of God. I observed, 'Under all civilized governments, teachers of religion are allowed to preach the divine law.' Towards the close, he used less haughty language than in the beginning, but utterly refused to reason with me."

About eight months subsequent to this, Mr. Kincaid was again summoned before the high court. On this occasion all the noblemen and an immense crowd of the common people were gathered together at the great court. As soon as Mr. Kincaid entered, the great *Black Book* was called for, and chapter after chapter was read, in which they had attempted a full delineation of his character. They said, in substance, that the *American teacher* had come to the Golden city; had stirred up great numbers of the people to despise the gods and religion of Burmah; was disturbing the public peace; was preaching a law which the king, the princes, and the nobles did not approve, and was giving books which taught a foreign religion—this, and a good deal more, they read, and no voice was heard but the reader.

At length they read a chapter to which Mr. Kincaid could not listen in silence. In substance it was this: "About seven months ago the American teacher promised to preach no more, and give no more books; but disregarding that promise, he had gone on ever since, preaching and giving the books in every direction."

Mr. Kincaid said—"I never heard of such a promise before. I promised to give no more of the Investigator; and the *Woon-gees* gave me permission to preach and give the sacred Scriptures."

No sooner had he said this, than a *Woon-gee*, in a boisterous and angry manner, said, "We know nothing about *your* books, and you promised to give *no books.*

Another said—" We know nothing about the distinction you make, and are determined to put down all preaching and all books which teach a foreign religion."

Mr. Kincaid remonstrated with them—told them about the Mahomedans and Papists, who were not molested; upon this, they became more vehement and rude, said these people did not preach and give books, and that he should not. They then called upon him to promise that he would preach no more and give no more books of any kind. Mr. Kincaid replied—

" I dare not promise."

" You must promise," said one of the council.

" I cannot, I dare not make such a promise: I fear God more than kings; and if you cut off both my arms and then my head, I cannot make such a promise."

" Remain quiet, and you can stay," said another.

" I dare not remain quiet; I came here to preach, and the command of God is to preach in all the world."

Half a dozen cried out furiously: " Send him away! send him away! he is not fit to live in the empire!"

Mr. Kincaid then made an appeal to the prince, the queen's brother; he listened to his story till he came to that part where he said the *Woon-gees'* promise induced him to rent a house at considerable expense. He then inquired how much money had been expended, and said the owner of the house should pay back the money. One of the ministers said—

"If we do not oppose you, we shall go to hell."

"But do not I preach the divine law?" inquired Mr. Kincaid.

"We dare not listen to you," said he, "we are afraid of hell."

"Thus," says Mr. Kincaid, in one of his letters, "they would have you think that from pious motives they set themselves against you. I have some hopes that this fit of bigotry will wear off, and the sun of prosperity again shine upon our path. I know the day of opposition will come; I know the empire of darkness is not to be overturned without much toil and suffering. We must not be discouraged; if driven from one point, we must seize upon another; and as good soldiers of the cross of Christ, we must continue struggling on the field of battle, till the triumphant shout is echoed through heaven and through earth, 'The kingdoms of this world have become the kingdom of Christ.' PRAY FOR US—*pray for the little band of redeemed souls in Ava.*'"

CHAPTER VIII.

THE GOSPEL IN THE GOLDEN CITY.

"Be not afraid, but speak, and hold not thy peace: for I am with thee, and no man shall set on thee, to hurt thee: for I have much people in this city."
Acts xviii. 9.

"O, 'tis pleasant, 'tis reviving
To our hearts, to hear, each day,
Joyful news, from far arriving,
How the gospel wins its way,
Those enlightening
Who in death and darkness lay."

FROM the preceding chapter, it will be seen that the labors of Mr. Kincaid in Ava were attended with no ordinary degree of anxiety. Almost from the hour of his arrival, however, he was cheered in his work with the clearest proofs of the divine blessing. His veranda was daily visited by persons of all classes, to the number of from one to eight hundred, many of whom seemed anxious to learn something about the new religion. Only three months after his arrival he writes in his journal: "The very thing that ought to rejoice me often troubles me; it is the numbers that are flocking to the veranda to read and hear the word of God. If I would, I could not resist the tide that is setting in. Our veranda is pretty well filled during the day, and sometimes forty or fifty come in at a time." About the same time, writing to one of his missionary brethren, he says: "It is time for us to be awake, and work while the door is open. More than two hundred were at the house yesterday. We have three promising inquirers. I really think the time of Burmah's deliverance is at hand. It is no passing cloud that hangs over the land: it is spreading in every direction; and the time must come, when showers large and rich will water this desert. Oh for that faith that heeds no mountains, and regards not the desert vallies."

With all this, however, he was not so sanguine in his hopes as to overlook the difficulties and trials which he subsequently encountered in the prosecution of his labors. "If you inquire," says he, "what is the prospect in Ava? will you be allowed to preach and give books, without being molested? I cannot answer this question; yet I do not think the government will lift its arm against the cross of Christ. We shall often be annoyed, I cannot doubt. In all ages the gospel has met with opposition. Can we expect it to spread in Burmah without violent opposition on the part of the priesthood and many of its rulers? For my part, I do not expect it. The sooner this war begins, the sooner will Burmah be saved. I long to see the flame kindled that shall purify this land of all its abominations."

To further this great work, on which his heart was set, Mrs. Kincaid devoted a considerable portion of her time to teaching, and doubtless access was thus had to many who, otherwise, would never have been reached. Still, the preaching of the gospel was relied on as the chief instrumentality, and it was not long till Mr. Kincaid was permitted to see evidence of its taking deep hold on the hearts of the people. Cases began to come to his knowledge which gave convincing proof not only of conviction of sin, but of saving faith in Jesus Christ. The first convert baptized was a woman about forty years of age. In giving an account of her conversion to Christianity, she said with great simplicity: "I know it is the true religion, because it takes away my pride, and makes me feel like a little child." And, being asked why she wished to be baptized, she replied—"I believe it is the appointed road for those who worship God?" Her baptism is described by Mr. Kincaid as a scene of peculiar beauty, and as an occasion of remarkable interest. Repairing to the Irrawaddy,

"We knelt down," he says, "upon the shore, and lifted up our hearts in thanksgiving to Almighty God for the tokens of his divine favor. *Mah Nwa Oo* was then buried beneath the wave, in obedience to her Saviour's will. How strikingly solemn this hour! How holy is this place! These waters, that have for ages been echoing the song of heathen worshipers, now listen to the voice of prayer rising to the throne of the Eternal. The spire of the royal palace gleams over our heads, and the walls of the Golden city fling their shadow upon the waters; but we heed it not. The King eternal, immortal, invisible, and only wise God our Saviour, has bid us plant his banners here. If God be for us, who can be against us? Several of the heathen were spectators of this scene; but no one offered the least insult in word or in action. Not a breath was heard but the voice of prayer, and the words of the divine commission.

We hope this may be the commencement of good days in Ava. Let waters break forth in this desert; let the wilderness blossom; let the Lord's house be established on the top of these mountains!"

Only a few days subsequent to this, they were again permitted to gather on the river shore, on the occasion of the baptism of *Moung Kay*, who, only four months previous, had been acknowledged one of the most popular preachers of Boodhism in the royal city. This man first heard the Gospel from the lips of *Ko San-lone*, one of Mr. Kincaid's native assistants. He, finding him one day explaining the sacred Pali to a large assembly of venerable men, sat down among them, and, when a favorable opportunity offered, he said to the preacher—"Have you heard that there is a God eternal, who is not, and never was subject to any of the infirmities of men ?"

"No."

"There is such a God, and his sacred word is in Burmah."

He then explained to him the leading doctrines of the Christian system. The truth pierced his heart. He asked for a book. The fifth day after he threw away his beads; forsook the pagodas; refused to bow to idols, and made no offerings to the priests. He read incessantly till the New Testament was gone through. He was especially affected with the view he there received of Christ's mediation, and at length, after carefully examining himself, he came forward, saying—

"I think I have a new heart. I see every thing differently from what I formerly did; every thing is so new that I can hardly sleep or eat."

The knowledge of his conversion, as might be supposed, created through the city no little stir, and his baptism was regarded as an event promising great advantage to the future interests of the mission.

The general attention awakened about this time towards the claims of the christian religion, is strikingly exhibited in the numerous cases of interest alluded to by Mr. Kincaid, in his journal. From this it appears that many men of distinction, and officers of government, as well as persons of humbler capacity and station, came often to inquire after the truth, or to bear their simple and honest testimony to the experience of its power on their souls.

On several occasions, by invitation, he visited the Palace, and was frequently sent for to converse with Prince Mekara, the most learned man, perhaps, in the empire. "At first," says Mr. Kincaid, "he seemed to be anxious only about science ; but, of late, he has become a student in the scriptures. He says, that St. Paul's Epistle to the Romans is wonderful beyond anything he ever read. I found him one evening comparing several passages together: he had the places marked which speak of the *law of faith*. I said,

'Your highness will be much gratified in reading the Old Testament scriptures.'

'Why ?' he inquired.

'Those writings give an account of the most wonderful events from the beginning of the world to the coming of Christ.'

'Be it so : this divine law must be more important than any history.' He then inquired—

'How is a person to know that he is a believer, and that he will be saved from all his sins ?'

I gave a short relation of my own Christian experience, particularly the peace I felt when the eyes of my understanding were first opened to see the beauty of the divine character. He listened with the most eager attention to every word. I urged the importance of venturing all on Christ, who alone can save us from our sins and present us pure and holy before the throne of God."

At a subsequent interview, this Prince said—"Every thing I read in your books I admire. It is a pure and holy religion, different from any other."

Secretly, there were many who gave similar testimonies. One, for instance, would say—"I see that this is the most excellent religion." Another—"The more I read of it, the more fully am I convinced that it is the true religion." And, another—"I believe in the religion taught by Jesus Christ. All other religions appear foolish and absurd when compared with this."

But some who even went further than this, and gave encouraging evidence of conversion, were wanting in the courage and faith necessary, under the circumstances, to a public confession of Christ.

"Fear," writes Mr. Kincaid, "keeps them from coming out openly on the side of truth; though many, in secret, declare their full conviction of the truth of the Christian religion."

From the first, Mr. Kincaid did not feel a doubt with reference to the ultimate success of this important mission, and though, in the prosecution of his work, much occurred to discourage his heart, we find him laboring on with a growing confidence in the final triumph of the Gospel. He saw clearly that there never before had been such an opportunity for making vigorous exertions for the salvation of Burmah, and, leaving all in the hands of God, he was resolved to labor unceasingly while he was favored with an open door.

"It is true," he says, "the government at times has been feverish, and on three or four occasions, has put itself into a threatening posture; yet all this has quickly subsided. Our heavenly Father has set open the door of hope, and the door of faith, so that, although there may be much that is trying, and sometimes even perplexing, we cannot but feel that a foundation is being laid for the introduction of great and manifold good into this benighted empire. The husbandman who enters a wild and cheerless forest, is obliged to toil long and painfully, before he can see a single field whitening for the harvest: he does not sit down, however, in hopeless sorrow. The hardy woodman's axe echoes through the gloomy forest, and, in process of time, there is an opening made, through which the light of day descends, and the fattening dews of heaven distil; then comes the delightful labor of casting in the seed, and gathering the joyous harvest. Shall we be less patient, less laborious, less hopeful? Shall we say this is the work of many long and painful years, and therefore abandon the labor in despair? Many long years may pass, before the reaper's song shall echo through these vallies ; yet that day will surely come."

Nor was that day long delayed, At the close of the first year spent in Ava a church of Christ had been planted, and during the three remaining years of his residence in that city, hundreds of thousands heard the word of eternal life, and though multitudes of these never went farther than to relinquish their belief in the superstitions of Gaudama, yet, doubtless, a great number silently accepted the faith of the Gospel, while others, who openly avowed their love to Christ, gave the most cheering evidence of having been made the subjects of a thorough spiritual change.

CHAPTER IX.

IN THE SHADOW OF THE HIMMALEH MOUNTAINS.

"To preach the Gospel in the regions beyond, and not to boast in another man's line of things made ready to our hand."—2 Cor. x: 16.

"We see new realms to truth expand,
Where truth was never known before;
Fields ripened for the reaper's hand,
Mines rich in everlasting ore."

No place in Burmah afforded such opportunities for the spread of the truth as Ava. Being the capital of the empire, and the seat of the Golden Presence, persons were to be met with here from almost every part of the realm; and what transpired in Ava, therefore, soon became known in the most remote portions of the land.

Availing himself of this advantage, Mr. Kincaid sought every opportunity of forming an acquaintance with those who came from distant provinces, that he might put into their hands the word of God, to be carried to the regions from whence they came.

In his intercourse with some of these strangers, Mr. Kincaid became deeply interested in a numerous people known as Shyans, and occupying the provinces on the northern frontiers of the empire. After obtaining all the information he could concerning the position of their country, he conceived the plan of a tour of exploration, to extend, if possible, as far as the borders of China and the frontiers of Assam. This design meeting the approval of his brethren of the Mission, he began at once to make the necessary arrangements for the excursion.

Hitherto no effort had been made, by any agent of the Christian church, to explore the field north and east of Ava; and, anxious to ascertain the extent of the population, the languages spoken, the character of the people, and the facilities for doing them good, Mr. Kincaid resolved to undertake the journey, and thus determine what could be done for the salvation of these millions of immortal beings who had never heard the Gospel. When first made acquainted with his plans, the government interposed serious objections, and forbad him passing through the upper provinces.

"The alleged reason," says Mr. Kincaid, "was that I had got permission to remain in Ava, and here I preached and gave books; but was not satisfied, and now wished to go through all the northern cities of the empire. This would not do; it was asking more than any foreigner had reason to expect. Without any delay I went to the Thoot dau. The spacious hall was crowded with hundreds of people, and the ministers were immersed in business. After a fatiguing half hour of elbowing and squeezing, I got through the dense mass of petitioners, secretaries, and petty officers, and found myself fairly in the presence of the lords of the land, with the queen's brother at their head.

'What does the American teacher want?' was the first question.

'Some days since, I made every arrangement to go on to Assam—my boat and every thing is ready; but to-day a message was brought that your lordships are opposed to my going by the way of Bomau and Mogaung; and my object in calling is to inquire into the ground of your opposition.'

'You must not go,' was the stern and prompt reply of two noblemen at the same time—one of them stroking down a huge tuft of beard that hung from the end of his chin, and putting on a countenance of great self-complacency—'we cannot consent to your going through our northern cities, and giving books to the people. If you wish to go to Assam, go by the way of Bengal; that is a good way.'

'But that would take me a whole year.'

'Let it take eight years,' said the haughty nobleman with the handful of black beard.

'You know I am a religious teacher, and should be allowed to go where I choose.'

'You must not go,' was reiterated by two or three. I made an effort to get from them the reason of their opposition, but it was unavailing. They appeared unwilling to get into any discussion, and I left them."

Subsequently he says, "I called on the Sa-lé prince (queen's brother.) He was seated in a hall of great extent; the roof was supported by a great number of gilt pillars, from thirty to forty feet in height. There were three landscape paintings hanging on the walls, not less than ten feet square, and on every side was evidence of wealth and eastern pride. The prince sat on an unpretending cushion, near the centre of the hall, dictating to a secretary a letter of instructions to the governor of Mogaung. Between one or two hundred officers, with their attendants, were sitting at a distance, on one side of the hall. I had been seated but a minute, when the prince observed me, and inquired the object of my visit. I related briefly my wish to go through the north of Burmah to Assam. He replied, 'that the ministers had taken up the subject, and were not agreed; and as long as the king's ministers were not of one mind, it would be impracticable.' Considerable conversation took place, but the main point was kept at a distance. Leaving the prince, I called immediately on Moung Yeet, an *atwenwoon*, whom I knew to be one of the principal opposers of my proposed tour. He was very affable. After hearing my statements, he said, frankly, though not haughtily—which is uncommon for a Burman of high rank—

'As one of the king's ministers, I have opposed your design; but now I understand it in a different light from formerly, and will lay it before his Majesty's officers.'

I tried, again and again, to get him to express his own opinion, but he was as cautious as if his life depended on keeping his own views concealed. I told him I had just seen the Sa-lé prince, and *he* made no objection, only said the ministers were not agreed.

'Did the prince say you might go?' inquired the minister, eagerly.

'No, he did not say that—he only said you, ministers, were not agreed; and now, if you and one or two more, who have opposed it, say *go*, all difficulties will be removed.'"

After many delays, however, he at length obtained a permit from government, and, on the 27th of January, 1837, embarked on the Irrawaddy in a boat provided and despatched in his charge, by the British Resident. The region of country through which he passed is described, in his journal, as one of uncommon beauty, and, as in other instances, the facts and incidents which transpired on the trip, served to give increased importance to Burmah as a field of labor, and to afford the most cheering prospect of its ultimate evangelization. It would be instructive to follow Mr. Kincaid in all the interesting features of this journey; the limits of the present chapter, however, forbid more than a brief reference to some of the most remarkable occurrences noted in his journal.

Aside from observations on the scenery through which they passed, and a close inspection of some ancient monuments of Boodhism found by the way, nothing of special moment occurred until the close of the third day, when, happening to stop for the night at a small village called Ya-tha-ya, it was discovered they had fallen upon a nest of robbers. Being too late, however, to proceed further, it was deemed prudent to prepare themselves against any attack, and Mr. Kincaid thus describes the measures adopted for their protection, with their success. "We had in the boat one musket and one pair of cavalry pistols. These I loaded with care. I placed the two oldest Burmans on the shore, with the musket, to keep watch by turns; had the boat so fastened that we could push off at a moment's warning; told the rest of the men to sleep, and, with the pistols lying beside me, I sat and watched till day-break. It was an uncomfortable night. About ten o'clock in the evening, a deep-toned gong sounded in the head-man's house. In a few minutes the villagers were together, talking boisterously, and sometimes angrily. The evening being clear and still, I could hear much that was said. The people were charged by the head-man to keep away from my boat. I also heard a good deal about spirits and opium. After an hour or so, all was still till about midnight, when the gong again sent forth its deep tones, echoing among the trees and rocks. In a few minutes I heard voices, and saw lights gliding along among the trees and cabins. All collected in the house of the head-man, and began talking, as before. My men on the shore inquired what was to be done. I told them to remain firm, unless a large number came down, and, in that case, come upon the boat immediately. It was an hour of deep anxiety; for no one who understood their language could mistake their character. Presently a tall man came down, and when within forty or fifty yards of us, my men hailed him and ordered him to stop. With an angry, coarse voice, he inquired why they stopped him, and was promptly told that I had so directed. I immediately spoke, and told him it would be unsafe to come nearer; that I had heard their language and witnessed their proceedings, and was fully prepared to resist them; that we were peaceable people, seeking only to benefit others, but should not tamely fall into the hands of lawless men. After looking at us a few minutes, he returned, and the villagers remained together all night, talking, singing, drinking spirits, and smoking opium."

On the afternoon of the next day Mr. Kincaid met

with a company of a very different character. "I came," says he, "upon a party of Shyans, twenty-five or thirty, male and female. They had built up their fires, and were cooking rice upon the shore. They were elderly people, had one large boat, and in it were provisions and various articles which make up what this people call *comfortable.* They were all dressed in coarse, dark blue cotton, and each one, whether at work or not, kept smoking from a pipe that had a stem three or four feet long. I let my boat go on, and remained half an hour in conversation with them, as most of them spoke Burman very well. They had come from a province about two hundred and fifty miles north-east of this, and were on a pilgrimage to places of reputed merit in various parts of the empire. I inquired,

'Why do you take so long a journey?'

One of them, whose face was wrinkled with age, though he was active and spoke with energy, replied, 'Our years are many, and we are going to visit all the most distinguished gods in the kingdom, that we may get peace and merit before death.'

'Have you failed of obtaining peace, by worshiping the gods in your own country?'

'Yes; and we have heard there are gods in Amarapúra, Ava, and Pagan, and that under them are relics of Gaudama, which possess indescribable power. To visit those places, and make offerings and prayers, is meritorious.' As he uttered these words, he laid down his pipe, looked me full in the face, and said, gravely and anxiously, 'What do you think—is this true?'

'No; it is all wrong. The gods you are going to see, are made of bricks and lime. Your offerings they cannot see; your prayers they cannot hear. The true God, who made heaven and earth; made you and me; gave us power to speak and think; gives us the three seasons—the warm, the cold, and the rainy; the eternal God, whose presence, power, and goodness are everywhere—that God is here, and hears all we say. He sees you and me, though with our bodily eyes we cannot see him. He is holy, free from sin, never sick, never sees old age, and never dies. He is God, the true God, and beside him there is no God.'

'Wonderful language'—'Extraordinary words,' replied half a dozen, with one breath—and then urged to hear more. Such a company of sober, venerable old men and women, entirely ignorant of the Being who made them, yet distinctly conscious of their accountability, is a scene deeply affecting."

Only a day or two after this, when at Kyouk-man, a village of fifty or sixty houses, there occurred an incident of thrilling interest. They had stopped there for the night, and having a little moonlight, Mr. Kincaid spoke to a number of the people gathered on the shore. After they had gone to their homes, and when all in the boat were asleep, "I was aroused, says Mr. Kincaid, "by a low voice, saying, 'Teacher, teacher;' and, starting up, I saw a man standing in the water, by the boat. Before I had time to make any inquiry, he began to apologize for disturbing me at that time of the night, and said he had been absent, and when he returned, a neighbor read to him a tract about God. Learning where he had got it, and fearing I might be gone before day-light, he resolved to come at once. It was very dark, but I could perceive by his voice that he was an old man. In few words I explained to him the character of God, and the provision God has made for the happiness of intelligent beings; and gave him a small book and two tracts. The poor old man went away, pouring forth a torrent of kind wishes, and saying he wished to understand this. For the first time in his life, he has heard there is an eternal God, who made the heavens and the earth. For the first time in his life, he has in his hand the gospel of peace."

The next night was spent at Kyouk-Kyih, a beautiful town, distinguished as the residence of the Governor of the province of Monhein. Calling upon the Governor, he received Mr. Kincaid in the most friendly manner, and gave him much information relating to the population of his province. He ordered dinner also, and though Mr. Kincaid remonstrated, telling him he had just dined, and would only take a cup of tea with him, it availed nothing. "A Governor," he said, "should be an example to others, and how would it appear, if I should let you go away without any expression of hospitality?" His wife and family were equally kind and pleasant with himself. Mr. Kincaid gave her a New Testament, and the Governor two tracts. They appeared much gratified with their gifts, and afterwards engaged freely in a long conversation on the subject of religion. The next morning, just as they were about to leave, the Governor's servants came down to the boat, bearing a present of rice, dried fish and vegetables.

In one village still further up the river, a large room in the head-man's house was filled with attentive hearers, and Mr. Kincaid continued reading and speaking to them until a very late hour. The conduct of the whole assembly was praiseworthy, and several of them said, they had never before supposed there was any religion in the world besides their own, worth thinking about; but, said they, this idea of an eternal God, and of a way to escape the punishment of hell, must be considered. A similar reception was given them at a number of towns both on the Irrawaddy and the Mogaung rivers—the head-man providing a room for a public service, and the people, flocking in and manifesting, in every instance, the most respectful attention.

At length, after being twenty-two days on the way and having traveled about three hundred and fifty miles from Ava, they reached Mogaung, the most northern city of Burmah. Here, beneath the shadow of the Himmaleh mountains, he found spreading before him the vast wilderness which separates Burmah from Hindostan, skirted by a territory crowded with people, and abounding in mines of amber and serpentine stone.

During the time spent here a thorough survey was made of the city, and several excursions were taken into the surrounding country. But after gathering all the information possible with reference to the extent and character of the population laying farther north, Mr. Kincaid was led to doubt whether there was any object of sufficient importance to warrant him in proceeding with his undertaking. But, beside this, he found it impossible to procure either provisions suitable for his journey, or men to accompany him, and having carefully weighed the matter, he, at last, concluded to set his face toward home. After taking an affecting leave of the Governor and his household, in which he repeated many things he had before told them of the eternal God, and of that futurity to which they were all hastening, he again embarked, and began with great rapidity to descend the river toward Ava. On reviewing this tour, together with the previous labors bestowed on Burmah,

Mr. Kincaid was led to the following encouraging reflections on the state and prospects of that mission:

"The prospect of enlightening and saving the people of this empire, has greatly increased in my mind, during my tour north. Not that I ever doubted its ultimate accomplishment, but obstacles appear less formidable, and ways of gaining access to the people less difficult. I may be too sanguine, 'too much inclined to look on the bright side;' but after four years' acquaintance with the government of Ava, and after traveling the whole length of the empire, visiting almost every town, and city, and village, on the Irrawaddy, from the Martaban gulf to the Himmàleh mountains, and forming an acquaintance with many of the provincial authorities, and learning with some degree of exactness, the extent, habits, and character of the various tribes of Burmah, it will be allowed that I have had at least an opportunity of forming some idea of what can be done. Eight years ago, no one would have supposed it possible that a missionary could go to Ava, and for four years preach the Gospel publicly, and baptize believers, and form them into a Christian church; that, as a teacher of religion, he would be received kindly into the houses of princes and noblemen; and that he would be allowed to travel about in the neighboring towns and villages, giving books, and preaching to the people. All this has been done, in the most frank and open manner. Twenty have been baptized, and formed into a church. On the Lord's day they meet, and sing, and pray, and hear the Gospel preached. Add to this, a great multitude have heard of God, and of the Mediator, and have read more or less of the Holy Scriptures. This, too, has been done in weakness, and with very insufficient means. Now, the field is better known—the prejudices, vices and habits of the people are better known. When all these facts are duly considered, there is much to inspire confidence in the use of those means which God has appointed for the conversion of the world. Obstacles there are, and will be as long as sin and idolatry exist, but they are not insurmountable, when encountered in the name and strength of Him who came to destroy the works of the devil."

CHAPTER X.

IN PERILS AMONG ROBBERS.

"The Lord is my light and my salvation; whom shall I fear? The Lord is the strength of my life; of whom shall I be afraid? When the wicked, even mine enemies and my foes came upon me to eat up my flesh, they stumbled and fell. Though an host should encamp against me, mine heart shall not fear."—Psalm xxii. 1–3.

"When exposed to fearful dangers,
Jesus will his own defend;
Borne afar 'midst foes and strangers,
Jesus will appear your friend;
And his presence
Shall be with you to the end."

THE perils and privations which Mr. Kincaid suffered in his passage down the Irrawaddy from Mogaung, form one of the most thrilling chapters of his wonderful history. The whole land was at this time in arms, all the horrors of anarchy and civil war had fallen upon the empire, and large bodies of men, under a sort of military organization, were prowling about the country—robbing and burning cities and villages, thus rendering all travel exceedingly dangerous.

He succeeded, however, in making a rapid passage down the river, to a point about two hundred miles from Ava, when he fell successively into the hands of two bands of banditti. His own language, used in a public address, though never before printed, will best convey to the mind of the reader an idea of his dreadful sufferings while in the hands of one of these savage hordes:

"We were passing gently down the stream," said Mr. Kincaid, "not, however, without frequent false alarms that robbers were near, for we had been informed at the last village where we stopped that we should soon have to pass through a mountainous region and a deep ravine, where the robbers were in great numbers. It was about 10 o'clock in the morning—I was lying under the cover of my boat engaged in reading, when one of my boys cried out, 'Teacher, the robbers.' I had so frequently heard this alarm, and as frequently found it to be false, for my people always stood in great fear, that I paid but little attention to it. Again he called out, 'Teacher, the robbers.' I looked out, and sure enough there was a boat full of armed men. I told one of the boys to hold up the musket, the only arms we had in the boat, and we carried this by the order of government, no boat being allowed to go up or down the rivers without a Burmese musket. The robbers, seeing that we were armed went back towards the shore shouting.

I sat down again unconcerned, and supposed that we should not again be molested. In a few minutes, however, my boys told me that more robbers were again approaching. This time I showed myself, and held up the musket, when they wheeled about with boats, and with loud shouting returned again towards the shore. I still had but little uneasiness, and was soon engaged with my book ; but only to give it up for increased and fearful danger. With a countenance manifesting great agitation, one of my boys cried—'O teacher, teacher, the robbers, the robbers!' and when I stood up, to my surprise I saw five or six large boats full of armed robbers, coming down upon us with great rapidity, yelling in the most awful and terrifying manner. I began to feel now that danger was indeed near, that I was unarmed, and all alone, for my affrighted and cowardly crew had laid themselves down in the bottom of the boat on their faces, crying in the most piteous manner, and I knew that I could obtain no help from them, and that resistance under such circumstances would be madness. When the robbers were within hailing distance, I said to them in Burmese, their own language, at the same time spreading out my hands—'Come, and take all we have got.' The only reply was—'Set down, set down,' and by this time there were not less than thirty musket pointed at my boat. I told them with as much firmness and apparent indifference as I could summon up in so trying a situation, that I would not set down, for I knew that if I attempted to sit down, they would have riddled me with their bullets. I told them not to fire, that I was a foreigner, and the Governor had promised his protection to me, and that if I was injured it would be at their cost. But I discovered that they were not to be intimidated either by threats or by the presence of a foreigner, for I had scarcely spoken the last sentence, when thirty or more bullets from their muskets were fired into my boat, but through a merciful and wonderful providence, without doing any of us the slightest injury. I heard some of the balls whiz past my ears, others struck the boat, and some fell into the water. The discharge of this volley of musketry was followed by the most piercing and horrid cries, and before I had time sufficient to recover from the shock of their fire, my boat was surrounded by these villainous robbers —and more than seventy spears encircled almost every part of my body, so that I was completely encased by steel points touching me. I could not move without feeling the points of their spears, but God was with me and sustained my courage. I did not lose my presence of mind. I was ordered into their boat, and they immediately commenced beating my four men and plundering the boat of its contents, calling out to me, 'Where is your money?' I gave them all I had. This, however, was not satisfactory.

Taken by the Robbers.

They immediately commenced stripping me. They took my hat, and shoes, and jacket, and vest, and were about to take my shirt and pantaloons, when I made some resistance, and told them that I would not be thus treated, but that they must take me before their chief man. By this time the boats had reached the shore. An armed guard of several men was placed over me; I was ordered to lie down, while the robbers went on shore to divide their plunder. Nor could I keep from smiling to see the ludicrous appearance that many of these wretched men presented. One had on a shirt, another a vest, another a jacket, and another a pair of pantaloons.

There had been many boats robbed during this and a few preceding days, from which they had secured a large amount of plunder and a great number of prisoners. Their deliberations turned, however, upon their foreign prisoner, and the course they should take with him gave them very great uneasiness. I could see from where I lay in the boat, that they were under considerable excitement, and that they contemplated getting rid of me in a manner that would cause the least trouble to their future security. I was not without my fears of the consequences, well knowing that they were in the habit of destroying their prisoners, whenever they had a suspicion that their escape would involve them in trouble. At the same time I felt that the superintending providence of God had faithfully preserved my life amidst scenes and dangers quite as fearful as the one in which I was now involved, and I had a faint hope that I should be preserved. In these trying circumstances, I lifted my heart to God in prayer for his continued protection. And his love and care were in a most wonderful manner exemplified.

After the robbers had divided their spoils equally, I was sent for to appear before the great man of the band, their chief. Not the least intimidated by the presence and the near contact of these wretched outlaws, these men of blood and carnage, whose very countenances were enough to cause the heart to sink, I passed with great apparent indifference through their numbers, until I came near to the chief, who was seated on the ground in the centre of the circle his men had made around him, and under a temporary awning, made by the large boat sail of coarse cloth, which was supported in the centre by a pole and secured at several points in the ground by their spears.

I sat down by this chief, and he entered into conversation with me freely as to who I was and where I was going, and what was my business; to these and many other questions of a similar character, I gave him correct answers, and solicited him to allow me and my boat's crew to go on our way, now that he had obtained all our property. I was buoyed up with the hope that he would grant my petition, as he listened very patiently to my conversation. He was a man dignified in his appearance, and possessed an open and benevolent countenance ; and several times while I sat by him, he betrayed, but for a moment only at each time, his sympathy for my condition.—Noticing this trait in his character, and knowing that he had the fullest confidence of his men, that his word was respected and his command supreme among them, I thought I would try how far I could gain upon him in order to obtain my liberty. Having been already deprived of my hat and jacket and shoes, and knowing how much I should suffer during the night from the cold dew and dampness of the weather, for I expected to remain out all night, I put my hand on the knee of the chief, and represented to him my destitute and exposed condition, and how I should suffer from the dewy and chilly night without sufficient clothing, and asked him to give me back one of my jackets ; and he immediately ordered one of his men to give me up a jacket, which order was promptly and without the least murmur obeyed. Finding some success, and sensible that this would not be enough to protect me during sleep, I again solicited him to return me a cloak, of cloth of a coarse material, but very comfortable and well made, which I had ordered from Bengal expressly for this journey just before I started, and which had not been much worn. Feeling satisfied that if I could obtain this I should be very comfortable at night, I looked around for it and discovered a fellow of most desperate appearance, having all the villainy of a cold-blooded murderer in his countenance, to whose lot it had fallen, sitting with it under him. When the chief asked for it he drew it still closer underneath him, as if to hide it, but I pointed it out to the chief, and he bid him give it up to me. The fellow, cursing, took it out, and it being enveloped in a piece of coarse stuff, he took hold of one end of the cloak, and finding that it was an article of more value than he at first supposed it to be, muttered dissatisfaction, and again placed it under him, and drew his sword with an apparent determination not to give up his prize and his share of the plunder without a struggle, at the expense of blood, and several of his wild comrades appeared to rally around him. I was not, however, to be deterred from my purpose with these threats ; I again called the attention of the chief to my cloak, but he turned away his head, as I spoke, which appeared to be a signal of dissatisfaction, as in a moment, a hundred swords were drawn, and with dreadful imprecations and yells, they rushed towards me, in great passion, as if to destroy me. This was enough. I saw that further entreaty was vain, and that I had created the dissatisfaction of the chief by my earnest and repeated applications for his clemency and favor. There appeared now to be great confusion among the robbers, who were walking about in terrible fury. Soon after this I was ordered to the boat under a strong guard, and was informed that the robbers were sitting in council and deliberating on my case whether to kill or release me.

It was a state of considerable anxiety and suspense to me, but I was relieved only to make uncertainty certain ; for when the council broke up, the youngest of my Burman boys, a lad about sixteen, approached me, overwhelmed in tears, and told me that the robbers had decided to behead me at sundown, the time of day when all Burman executions took place. The knowledge of my sentence was almost more than I could bear. For a few minutes I was completely overpowered, a cold perspiration came over me, my breathing was short and interrupted, my mouth became parched, and my tongue seemed to cleave to the roof of my mouth. It was not so much the fear of death, but the character of my death. I looked upon the dreadful place in which I was called to die, and the nature of the circumstances by which I was surrounded,—alone, among a band of fierce robbers, outlaws, and murderers ; their cold-blooded determination to take my life without a single exciting cause for convicting me ; no friend to communicate with, and to tell the state of my mind, none, perhaps, to carry the tidings of my death to Ava, to the mission, and to my family—for it was very doubtful then whether any of the Burmans who were with me would ever escape—the sensations were dreadful, and I can scarcely bear even now to think upon them. However, I recovered in a very few minutes from this state of mental despondency, and thought—what is this? it is nervousness, it will never do, I must rally. If this is death, I must meet it with Christian firmness. I am still in the hands of my heavenly Father, who has oftentimes preserved me, and why need I fear what man can do unto me; they can kill the body, but they cannot destroy the soul. I know I must die, and if this is the time and the manner which God has appointed for my departure, I do resign myself into his Almighty hands, and I trust, come what may, it will all be for his glory. Thus I struggled with my feelings, and reasoned with myself, until I gained the mastery, and until entire composure and reconciliation to my fate settled over my senses. I had nothing now to do but wait the time fixed upon, which was within two hours, for my execution. But man appoints, and God disappoints. I watched the fleeting moments as they sped by, and I could not keep my eyes off my executioners, who appeared to be engaged in an angry war of words; they became louder and louder, and I found, by catching a word now and then of their conversation, that they were divided in opinion as to my sentence of death.

A faint hope stole over me that the hand of God was about to be extended for my preservation, and I uttered a prayer for relief. The robbers drew their swords, looked fierce, and seemed ready to plunge them into each other, so violent was their anger.

In a little while, from some strange circumstance, they resolved among themselves, after having reversed the decision of my death at sundown, to go to a village a few miles above and plunder its inhabitants. Before nightfall, to my great relief, there was not a single man of the bandit on the ground, and their prisoners were left alone unsecured. No sooner had they departed than I determined, feeble and exhausted as I was, to make my escape, and told my men that as soon as we could get something to eat, for there was plenty of rice left in the boats, we would take our boat, get it into the current of the river, and in the darkness of the night make our escape beyond the fear of detection."

CHAPTER XI.

DANGER AND DELIVERANCE.

"Thy God whom thou servest continually, he will deliver thee."--Dan. vi. 16

"Just in the last distressing hour,
The Lord displays delivering power;
The mount of danger is the place,
Where we shall see surprising grace."

AFTER effecting an escape, as described in the last chapter, nothing occurred to interrupt their security until just at the dawn of day, when they saw a village about a mile ahead, and as they approached it their ears were assailed with the most terrific yells, and a number of armed boats were seen putting off from the shore, to head them as they came down the stream. They were again in the hands of robbers. They soon overhauled them, and four young men well armed jumped into the boat, and each one seized like young tigers upon their prey. They got hold of Mr. Kincaid's stock and collar, and dragged in every direction so furiously that he was almost choked, and became so far insensible that he could not tell what he was doing. In this state, and perhaps with a death-struggle, he threw up his arms and released himself from their grasp. This, however, only added to their fury, and, seizing him again, they tore off his stock, his collar, jacket, shirt, pantaloons and shoes, leaving him without a vestige of clothing. Recovering from the shock of this brutal treatment, he stood on his feet before his fierce and cruel enemies. They then commenced tying his arms after the manner of Burmese criminals. Mr. Kincaid was determined, however, to resist this treatment, and told them that they should not tie him, that he never had been tied, and that he should resist being tied until death. With this they set up a loud laugh and grinned awfully at him, but did not persist in tying him. When they reached the shore, they dragged him along some yards from the place of landing, and there made a ring in the sand around where he stood, and told him for his life's sake not to step beyond it. A guard of armed robbers, numbering from fifteen to twenty, surrounded this ring, and thus left him scarcely any chance for escape.

One of his Burmans, who saw and felt for his exposed condition, took off his waist cloth, tore it in two, and handed him the one half, which he secured around his waist, and in this dreadfully exposed condition, without an article of food or drink except what he begged from the women of the village, as they passed and repassed down to the river for water, did he remain six days and six nights, without any shelter from the scorching heat of the midday sun, or the cold damp air of the night. But besides this he did not know what would be his fate from day to day, or from hour to hour, and he was continually harassed by impertinent questions and the cowardly threats of his cruel tormentors, who left no means unemployed to make his situation as miserable as possible.

During the time that he remained a prisoner here, all his four boatmen and three of his boys made their escape in the night. The fourth and last one, Tha-oung by name, came to him on the third day, and observing him casting his longing eyes in the direction of Ava, Mr. Kincaid knew that he wished to inform him of his intention to run away. He would walk all around him at a distance, and then would come near, appearing as if he wished an opportunity to speak to him, and yet it seemed as if he could not bear the idea of going away and leaving his teacher to die by the hands of the robbers. At last, making his way to him, he sat down by his side and wept like a child, telling him that he intended to make his escape that night, that the others had run away, and it was the only chance he had to regain his liberty. Mr. Kincaid told him to go, and that if he ever reached Ava and the mission station, to give all the information he could about him. He gave him also good council, told him never to forsake his profession, to be a good boy, and then they might hope to meet again. It almost broke his heart when he was leaving, and, after going a short distance he stopped, and returning, said—"*Teacher, I will never leave you, but will stay by you until I die.*" This resolution Mr. Kincaid endeavored to dissuade him from keeping, but it was of no avail, his mind was made up to remain as a prisoner. On the very next day, however, this faithful boy was selected from among the prisoners to go into the interior, as the servant to one of the petty chiefs and a number of the gang. Nothing more was heard of him until two or three months afterwards, when he returned to Ava. Mr. Kincaid now thought seriously of making his escape, but not without counting the cost of the hazard. He knew that he was about two hundred miles from Ava—that he should be obliged to avoid the river and the villages lying along its margin, as the whole country was in a state of anarchy and confusion—that the whole way down, indeed all the region around, was infested with hordes of banditti, and that he should be obliged to take to the mountains and the mountain passes, through an unbroken country, which had perhaps seldom, if ever, been trodden by a human being. Hour after hour he watched the mountains in the distance, to see if he could possibly discover any path or any hope of relief. But while dreading the perils to be encountered, he thought if death had any preference, it was in the effort to escape, rather than by remaining to die by the hands of his cruel captors. After much reflection, therefore, his mind was made up to leave, and he set about making some preparation for the journey. Being altogether destitute of clothing, and beginning to feel sadly the effects of this constant exposure, he endeavored to single out that man of all his guard whose countenance displayed the greatest amount of benevolence, determining to make advances, and, if possible, obtain his favor. Having selected his man, he spoke to him and reasoned with him about his exposure, telling him how unaccustomed he was to go without clothing, and to sleep without a covering at night. In this way he soon won upon him, so that he went and brought him an old piece of sail-cloth, and afterwards the pantaloons of which they had stripped him when first taken a prisoner. Mr. Kincaid was now made up, and, fearing lest his frequent importunities would awaken suspicion, he deemed it best not to ask for any thing more, and resolved to start on his perilous journey the first convenient moment that offered for making an escape.

During the six days that Mr. Kincaid was detained among these robbers, parties were sent off every day to plunder travelers and to rob in the neighboring towns, and often, in the night, the sky would be lighted up from the flames of burning villages. These parties, after robbing and burning the houses and barns, would drive into their haunt large flocks of cattle, and roast them, and feast, and drink, and smoke the whole day.

He was not imprisoned more than twelve feet from where the robber chieftain sat, and from morning until night parties of the bandit were bringing in women and children, and the chief would examine them in order to learn where their valuables were buried —it being the custom of these people to hide their gold and jewels in jars in the earth, for fear of fire and thieves. If these women refused to tell where their valuables were buried, they were shamefully treated and cruelly beaten. They would strip them, throw them on the ground, tie their hands and feet together, and then, with large rattans, a robber would scourge these females in a most unmerciful manner. Sometimes, even if they would yield from their intense suffering, and tell where their gold was hid, they would go on beating them because the robbers would say that was not all. Many of these women, though their sufferings were dreadful, bore the scourging with astonishing fortitude. The robbers did not wish to put them to death, but to inflict torture ; and after whipping them until their backs were torn and lacerated, they would take their spears and pierce holes in their bodies half an inch in depth, and after making thirty or forty of these stabs, they would take pieces of split bamboo, and dip one end in melted sulphur and stick the other end into the punctures they had made in the bodies of these poor captive women, and then light them as tapers, and this they seemed to take great delight in doing. During these horrid cruelties, Mr. Kincaid was obliged to sit and witness them. He would close his eyes, but he could not shut his ears to their lamentations, and the cries of their children, who had to look on and behold these monsters beating and abusing their mothers.

On the sixth day he witnessed a scene of cruelty far surpassing all the others. It was a case of scourging of a female who had with her seven children. She was taller than most Burmese women,—of slender frame, and had a fine, intellectual countenance. With a dignified nobleness she stood before her captors, and with an expression of defiance refused to answer their questions. He could not help looking upon her and her seven children clinging around her, but with intense interest. She was then beaten by a robber—a thick, muscular man, who could strike with great power. The chieftain would cry out—"Strike quick," and then he would lay it on with vengeance. Her hair falling down over her back, which was bare, was clotted with blood and her face was cut unmercifully. Every blow, Mr. Kincaid expected, would be the last. Finally her head fell on her shoulder, her eyes were fixed, her lips pale, and she rolled over on the ground. Death had at last released her. Her eldest child, a beautiful girl, who held the infant in her arms, and her five brothers and sisters wept bitterly, when they found their mother was dead. This girl laid the babe at her feet, and fell down upon the body of her mother, uttering the most piteous and piercing cries of anguish—repeating again and again, "Mother, don't die and leave us."

Looking around on these fiends in human shape, Mr. Kincaid waited to see if there was one who would speak a kind word to these orphan children, but among them all there was no one to pity. Indeed, one of them violently kicked the poor child, to get out of the way, and she fell over speechless, on the ground. This was too much, he could bear such brutality no longer—the feelings of his nature were aroused; he was overcome with revenge; he was conscious of but a single maddening sensation, and that was to get the life of the monster. But, rising to his feet, and finding himself tied, in a sort of despair, he called him by every epithet that human language could invent, wholly indifferent as to what might be his fate. To tantalize him the whole band burst out into a loud laugh. His mind was now made up to escape that night. The remainder of the day he kept a close watch on his guard and on the mountains.

The night drew on, and as usual the guard took it in turn to sleep. But there was no rest for him. He was between hope and fear as to the success of his escape, knowing well that if detected his life would be the forfeit. It was long after midnight before he ventured to stir, and when he did so, it was with the utmost caution. He listened—they were all quiet. He rose on his hands and feet—he crept slowly and softly to where they lay. Nothing caused him to startle but the heavy snoring of one of the guards. He moved carefully around him, scarcely breathing. Now he was outside the guard, and quickening his pace, he hurried on, and on, until he was beyond the precincts of the village. Soon he reached the skirts of the forest. He entered the jungle—and now breathing more freely, he felt that he had escaped, and that, before morning, he should be far beyond their reach. A heavy fog arising in the night facilitated his escape ; and about the dawn of day he reached the mountains. By this time he was much exhausted ; what with anxiety, and loss of sleep, and hunger, and exposure, and the fatigue of traveling, he felt it impossible to take another step, and after returning thanks to God for his great deliverance, and asking his protection on his journey and while he rested, he threw himself on the earth, and soon fell into a sweet sleep. When he awoke, to his surprise, the sun was near meridian ; and starting up, he hurried on as fast as possible, through a dense and tangled forest, which had never before, perhaps, been trod by the foot-steps of man. That day he traveled without water, but about sundown he espied a little ravine, and traced it, until at last he came to a muddled spring of water, the top of which was covered with a dark red-colored scum; but being thirsty and exhausted, it was not a time to be particular, and after partaking of the remaining stock of rice, he laid down on his face, pushed away the scum with his hand, and putting his mouth into the water, drank, until his burning and raging thirst was entirely quenched. Without rising, he rolled over, fell into a deep sleep, and never awoke until the sun was up.

Stiff in all his limbs, and with feet blistered and bleeding, he urged himself to move on again, but it was a painful task; for an hour or two he was obliged to move slowly and with great care. More than once he felt as if nature would sink, and that he must give up, and lay down and die in the deep recesses of the forest, far away from friends, alone, unbefriended, and beyond the reach of man. The idea of so awful a death preyed upon him, and he was driven to make another effort—a deep struggle took place between his two natures, and forcing himself to a desperate resolve, he seemed to be clothed with new strength, and was nerved to go forward. Toward the latter part of the afternoon, having descended a mountain pass, he came into the plain, and saw, at a distance, the hamlet of a Burmese peasant. He was not long in reaching the cottage, and making his situation known by telling his tale of sorrow. The old man invited him into the house, and his wife sat before him a large dish of cold boiled rice. After this welcome meal, he laid down on a mat and slept. In the morning he again resumed his journey—traveling nearly all day before he came within sight of any village. At last he reached a spring, and after drinking he laid down, waiting with much anxiety for the women of the village to come and fill their jars. He had not laid long until he saw a woman coming with her jar for water, and as she approached, he spoke to her kindly and bade her not to be afraid, telling her that he had been taken by robbers, and had made his escape, and all he wanted was a mouthful of rice.—She told him to remain where he was, that there were many robbers around the country, and should he enter the village, suspicion would be created. Filling her jar, she returned, and in a short time came back with a meal of cold boiled rice. After giving thanks, he partook of his solitary meal, and again laid down and slept undisturbed until morning. On resuming his journey, it was several hours before he could walk with any degree of satisfaction, owing to his stiffness and the soreness of his feet. Nothing particular occurred on that day's journey, until about the close of the day, when, as he reached the brow of a hill, he came suddenly on a banditti, who were taking their evening meal. They were horrid looking men, and he was much alarmed at the unexpected sight. But, preserving his presence of mind, he determined to walk on as if wholly indifferent to the surrounding scene. As he neared them, and when abreast of them, one and another stretched out their necks and looked at him with a fiendish grin, but no one seemed willing to leave his meal to approach him. Thus he passed on, not venturing to look back lest he might attract their further notice and suspicion; and, when out of sight, he fell on his knees, and returned thanks for another merciful deliverance.

He pursued his course, after another night's rest, through a country only partially settled with Burmans, and would here and there meet with a cleared patch of ground, tilled by some poor natives, who would hide themselves as he passed, as though they were afraid of the very sight of man. He had until now been pursuing his journey eastward toward the Shan country, and, having been five days on his journey, he took a circuitous route and struck for the Irrawaddy, coming out just at nightfall near a little village about thirty-five or forty miles above Ava. He did not dare to approach the village, but avoiding it, he soon found a path that led to a point in the river where the females came for water, and as he knew they would soon come down with their jars, and remembered that he had never been refused food from the hand of a Burmese woman, he laid himself down in the sand, exhausted with fatigue, and pressed with hunger, near by where they would have to pass. He had not been long in this situation, when he saw approaching two females, from whom he obtained a large pan of boiled rice. After making a rich meal on this, he laid down, once more, and slept, unmolested, until the break of day. Upon awakening he immediately started on his way, and had not gone far, when he met with a man whose face he had seen before in some of his excursions along the river, and, with the promise of an exorbitant price, he was induced to carry him in his boat to Ava.

The four native brethren who had been taken prisoners with him, but who had contrived to escape, returned some weeks afterwards. They reported that they had suffered much for want of food, and, when driven by want into a village, they had been captured by another horde of banditti, and even after escaping from these had passed through many privations and dangers. They had mourned for Mr. Kincaid as dead, and no language could express the joy and astonishment they felt at again meeting him.

CHAPTER XII.

LABORS IN TENASSERIM.

"Now thanks be unto God, which always causeth us to triumph in Christ, and maketh manifest the savor of his knowledge by us in every place."

2 Cor. ii. 14.

"In the deserts let me labor;
On the mountains let me tell
How he died—the blessed Saviour—
To redeem a world from hell."

AFTER passing through the fearful perils narrated in the two preceding chapters, Mr. Kincaid reached Ava on the 11th of March, and found the city filled with the most distressing alarms. Prince Thur-ra-wa-di had risen against his brother, the king, and, after a terrible struggle, he succeeded in dethroning him. The whole country now presented a scene of desolation and misery truly heart-rending. The whole length and breadth of the empire was laid waste. Half of the population had been robbed, and war was raging in all the distant provinces. The capital and neighboring cities, moreover, had by this time been invested with his armies, and such was the danger which threatened the mission families, that it was deemed prudent to accept the invitation of Colonel Burney, the British Resident, and take up their temporary abode under his roof; here they remained for the space of six days.

During the continuance of the civil war, and after the new king ascended the throne, sanguine hopes had been cherished that the prospects of the mission would become more than ever encouraging. The character of the Prince seemed to warrant such expectations. He had always sought for intercourse with foreigners, and had been remarkable for the liberality of his opinions. He had expressed, also, his disapprobation of the exclusive, jealous policy of the Government, and, whenever it came in his way, had spoken disapprovingly of its harassing and vexatious course toward Mr. Kincaid.

But, alas! with all these grounds of hope, they were doomed to a sad and sudden disappointment. About the middle of May intimations were given that the king had expressed himself averse to the American teachers, and that he should order a discontinuance of their labors. Hearing this, Mr. Kincaid sought, at once, an interview with the king. His majesty received him with evident marks of kindness, and gave him to understand that he was not personally unfriendly to him. "But," said he, "I am now king of Burmah, and am, therefore, *tha tha na da ya ka,* (defender of the faith) and must support the religion of the country. You must give no more of Christ's books." This he said before the whole assembled court, and added many expressions signifying that the royal will must not be trifled with.

Under these embarrassing circumstances, and apprehending war in consequence of difficulties between the English and the new Burman authorities, it was determined best to leave the capital for a time, and wait patiently until things should become more settled and quiet.

Leaving Ava on the 17th of June, they reached Rangoon on the 6th of July. Upon their arrival there, it was found that the missionaries of that station had already gone to Maulmain, in consequence of the threatening aspect of the revolution, and the decrees which had been issued by the viceroy of the province.

Early in the following month, Mr. Kincaid proceeded to Maulmain, and thence to Tavoy, with the intention of laboring in the Tenasserim province, until the state of the country should warrant his return to Ava. From Tavoy he hastened to the city of Mergui, the place which he had selected as an inviting field for temporary labor. While making this his home, however, the greater proportion of his time was employed in visiting and preaching at points of interest in the surrounding country, and, wherever he went, a blessing seemed to attend his efforts. In one village, for instance, twenty-five miles distant, he found the people eager to listen to the word of life, and during his sojourning among them, a congregation, numbering from sixty to one hundred souls, would usually gather and join with interest in the exercise of worship. At every successive visit made to this place, he was permitted to see the fruit of his labors, and, in a short time, he had the unspeakable privilege of breaking bread to a church numbering thirty-six rejoicing converts. Among other excursions, he made a visit among the islands some thirty miles from the Tenasserim coast, and about one hundred and fifty miles south of Mergui. Here he found a people in the most abject poverty and degradation. The account he has given of his brief sojourn among them cannot be read but with feelings of the deepest interest and pity.

"The islands," says he, "are all densely wooded, and of all sizes and forms. Some of them are low and very level, others have bold rocky shores, and rise into mountain ridges. The climate, too, must be delightfully pleasant. One cannot help exclaiming—'This is a beautiful world.' The ocean, on every side, spotted with a thousand green islands and islets, all beaming with existence—'Man alone is vile.' Those modern infidels, who dream of perfection if they can only wipe out all systems of religion, might find a splendid field here, all cultivated to their hands. I am now surrounded by about three hundred souls, men, women, and children, entirely free from all religion. They have no God, no temple, no priest, no liturgy, no holy day, and no prayers. In their domestic habits they are free from all conventional rules. They are very poor, too, have no house, no garden, no cultivated field, no domestic animals but dogs. I never saw such abject poverty, such an entire destitution of all the comforts of life.

I have remained on this little island five days, and every morning and evening, sitting on the sea-beach, have taught this poor, degraded people, the knowledge of God. I have resorted to every method of instruction, in order to reach their understanding; with how much success, is known only to the Great Teacher, who is the *true light.* Of God and immortality they had never heard; so much the more they appeared to be interested. Two evenings a large number of them remained till after 9 o'clock. Last evening I urged them to pray to the living God, of whom they had now heard, and in doing so, uttered several short prayers, or rather sentences, that they might the better understand me. Their attention was greatly arrested, and several immediately asked to be taught to pray. I taught them a short prayer, containing three or four sentences, and then asked them if they would forsake all sin and serve the great

God, who made heaven and earth. Some eighty or a hundred immediately replied, 'I will'—'I will.' I told them about the Karens, their conversion to God, and learning to read. They urged me to come and live on one of their islands; said they would all learn to read and become Christians."

Not less remarkable is the narrative he has furnished of his passage over the Tenasserim Mountains. Starting from the village before alluded to, where his labors had been so signally blest, he arrived, after a march of six hours, at the foot of the mountains, and put up for the night. Here he found two families, living in solitude, and among them, to his great joy, were four persons whom he had previously baptized. They gave him a most cordial welcome, spread a mat in an open veranda, brought water for washing and drinking, dressed a fowl for his dinner, and did every thing that kindness and Christian courtesy could dictate. The next morning he ascertained that while only four in these two houses had been baptized, there were not less than sixteen who believed in Christ, and gave satisfactory evidence of a change of heart. After taking an affectionate leave of these families, Mr. Kincaid thus describes, in graphic language, their toilsome journey, with some of its incidents:

"We set off in Indian file, for more than three hours wending our way along the bed of a mountain stream, sometimes only two or three feet deep. On either side the mountains rose up to a great height. In many places the stream is filled with brush and fallen trees, over which we had to climb ; though this was not always practicable, and we were obliged to creep on our hands and feet for fifteen or twenty yards together. After leaving this stream, or rather getting to the head of it, we ascended the high range of mountains which stretch along from north to south between the Tenasserim and the ocean. I was obliged to lie down on the ground several times, completely exhausted, before I got to the top. The mountains are irregular, precipitous, and covered with a dense forest. We traveled about four hours amidst these wild ragged mountains, often having no other path than that made by wild elephants and tigers. This is their own undisputed territory, and if one may judge by their tracts and paths, they are very numerous. Monkeys too range these wild regions in countless numbers. There is one kind very large, and without tails. The Karens tell me they are bold and savage, often attacking travelers, if not more than two together. When surrounded by great numbers of these animals, urging each other forward to an attack, by the most deafening yells, the only security is in setting fires, of which they, like other wild animals, are afraid. For ten or twelve days past we have had thunder storms every evening, preceded by heat that is nearly suffocating. The thunder is so loud and so constant, that it is difficult making a person hear only a few feet distant. About 4 o'clock the clouds began to gather in dense black masses; and, as the Karens tell me the storms are much more severe in these mountains than on the plains below, we concluded to halt for the night. Every effort was made to provide a shelter from the rapidly gathering storm. I was so weary it was impossible to render any assistance. We had a very comfortable shelter in less than an hour. Before our dinner was prepared, the storm came down, and except on one or two occasions, I never saw such a storm before. The whole atmosphere appeared to be a living mass of fire. There was a continued roar of thunder, mingled, almost every breath, with sharp, deafening peals, like the discharge of heavy artillery. The rain too was poured out in torrents, from which our leaves afforded us but a partial refuge. The awful grandeur of the scene, however, banished all thought of inconvenience and discomfort. Time passed unnoted; hours appeared to be minutes; there was no room for levity, and no room for sadness. The huge masses of clouds, hurrying on, and rolling up and down the sides of lofty and ragged mountains, the blazing atmosphere, the incessant roll of thunder, and the torrents of rain, accompanied with strong gales of wind, altogether formed a scene most impressively sublime.

In the morning I found two of my people suffering with a burning fever. One of them, a fine young lad, after making two or three efforts sunk down upon the ground, quite unable to walk. I had slight fever all night, but was very well in the morning. We set off at an early hour, and after eight hours' march, reached the Tenasserim, one hundred and forty or one hundred and fifty miles above Mergui. Our journey to-day, as yesterday, has been amidst the wildest scenes of nature, most of the way without the least evidence that any human being had been there before us. I suppose one-half the distance we walked in the channel of a stream, having, some part of the way, a most welcome sandy bottom, with only a few inches of water ; then again, rocky and precipitous, with occasional deep basins, taking us nearly to the chin in water. Tracks of the rhinoceros, elephant, tiger, deer, wild hog and monkey, are everywhere seen. Their hard-beaten and frequent paths give one a fearful idea of their number. There is here no spot of barren earth. Vegetation is every where seen, in all its wildest luxuriance. We are all quite happy to get over the mountains to this pleasant little village. Our reception has been so cordial that we quite forget the hardships of the past three days.

This village, or rather hamlet, stands on the west side of the river, on high level ground, with an extremely fertile soil. The river is about three hundred yards wide. The chief has visited me two or three times in Mergui, and for a month past has been expecting my arrival. Some time since he built a zayat, in which himself and neighbors meet on the Sabbath and worship the Christian's God. There are five houses, having thirty-two or thirty-three souls. But two or three miles distant, are other hamlets, sitting in the shades of death, and either enemies or ignorant of God. At early candle-lighting all came to hear the gospel. I preached from 'And as Moses lifted up the serpent in the wilderness, even so must the Son of man be lifted up.'

The next day was the Sabbath, and having met early to spend a little time in prayer and singing, messengers were afterwards sent off to inform two or three distant hamlets of my arrival, and try to bring them out to hear the blessed gospel. After breakfast spent some time in examining candidates for baptism. Preached at half past ten, and then resumed the examination. Four were received and baptized in the Tenasserim, about four o'clock. * * *

After commending this little church to the care of God and to the word of his grace, and promising, if possible, to send them a school teacher, and also to visit them again myself, I turned away most reluctantly from this bethel. During the day visited two hamlets, with, I believe, nine or ten houses, and preached Christ to the people. Put up for the night on a sand-bank, as the men dare not fasten to the shore on account of tigers. The day before yesterday, a poor Karen near us, was seized and carried off, though seven or eight men were with him and made every effort to save him. The whole country is wild and mountainous, covered with forest trees of great size.

Yesterday saw about thirty Karen houses, and in two places spent some time in preaching the gospel. To-day found about as many more widely scattered houses on the bank of the river, and in one place found a pleasant little zayat, built for the service. Here are two persons baptized by Br. Mason, and four or five more who keep the Sabbath and pray. I read and explained the scriptures for some time. Three of them can read a very little, and I supplied them with the gospels of Matthew and John, and with hymn-books. They besought me earnestly to come and spend a week with them, so that many more might hear the way of life. God is surely among this people. They are the 'good ground' spoken of by the Saviour, while the Burmans are the 'way-side.

Several miles from this zayat, lives the greatest Karen chief in this province. I visited him. He has a very large house, and, for a Karen, is wealthy. He soon learned who I was, and affected great indifference to my message ; put on haughty airs ; said that Christ's religion was turning the heads of his people, and hinted that he was not so insane as to forsake the old paths trodden for ages by his fathers. He spoke Burman fluently and correctly, which is no small attainment for a Karen, as they can never pronounce a word that ends with a consonant. I heard him patiently, and commended the principle of adopting new sentiments with extreme caution, and never without clear evidence of their truth, and then added, 'Your fathers were more enlightened than mine, for they knew the name Jehovah, and in every age rejected idolatry. I preach to you now the Jehovah of your fathers, and offer you instruction from the book He has given.' Without allowing him to reply, I read from several places in the New Testament, and 'appealed to his own apprehension of truth, if these things did not commend themselves to his conscience.' His airs were gone ; with altered tones of voice, he acknowledged that he often thought the religion of Christ was true. He said, that some months since, he had a child very ill, and made offerings to the nats, but his child died. He made a solemn promise then, that he would never make such offerings again ; but said he had tried to give up drinking spirits and could not, and so could not be a disciple of Christ. I urged on him the importance of believing in Christ, as the only way to obtain eternal life. He followed me down to the waters, with many invitations to come again."

In the autumn of 1838, Mr. Kincaid began to feel very desirous of returning to his labors at Ava, and having succeeded in supplying his place at Mergui, he hastened to Maulmain, with the hope of finding it practicable to proceed at once to the Royal city.—"I long," said he, "to be there. My whole heart is there, and if I had consulted my own judgment exclusively, I should have been there some months ago."

As it did not appear judicious, however, for him to return, he sent up two of the disciples—Moung na Gau and Moung Tha Oung, to visit the church at Ava. Shortly after this, Mr. Kincaid received the subjoined letter from one of the converts who had remained at the capital; and though the intelligence it brought was in most respects exceedingly cheering, still it awakened no little sorrow from the fact that it revealed a state of things which compelled a longer absence from his chosen field.

"MY BELOVED TEACHER KINCAID—After reaching Ava, and finding my parents, I lost no time till I had found out the residence of all the disciples. Some of them have removed to Amarapura, and they are so scattered that they do not meet oftener than once in a month, some once in two months. Soon after getting to Ava I wrote a letter, and on desiring to take it to the English resident's, the Burman officers forbade me, saying, 'there was no permission to go or send a letter. Besides this, a priest went merely to see the English, and was seized and taken away to execution, so that I did not dare to send you a letter. Now, feeling a great desire to write you, I have gone secretly to a foreign merchant, and he will send the letter—after this I hope to be able to send you letters often. Not long after getting to Ava, Ma-ee,* the daughter of Ko Shwa-nee, died. After this, Moung Moung† died of a fever, and was ill only three days. The disciples here are like sheep without a shepherd, and are anxiously looking for the time when the teachers can come. I wish much to return to you, teacher, but my father and mother are old and very infirm, and cannot get about well, so that I must remain and support them by my labor. When the disciples meet, they consult together about fleeing from this city to Maulmain, but as yet dare not make the attempt. The disciples remain strong in the faith of Christ, and pray to God continually. The writer, Ko Shwa-nee, is perseveringly preaching the gospel. Men-dong-gee and Moung You come to Ko Shwa-nee's house every three and four days, and reason with him about the law of God.

To the beloved teacher,

From MOUNG OO DOUNG."

* *Ma-ee* was one of Mrs. Kincaid's school girls.

† *Moung Moung* was a brother of great promise

"I, Moung Oo Doung—How much I remember, and how much I love the teachers and their ladies, I cannot fully express. In the night season I dream about them, and weep much. Thus ardently loving each other in this world, although separated, when we remove to the future world, in the heavenly kingdom, and meet face to face in the presence of God, all former anxiety will be forgotten. Whether enjoying much prosperity in this life, or suffering much adversity, let not the mind be elated with the one, or cast down at the other, even as by diligent perseverance in divine things we have hope of eternal bliss and happiness. My beloved teacher, I purpose to write in this letter about worldly events and about the heavenly religion in the city of Amarapoora. Concerning the intelligence which a foreign merchant in this city gave you,—if you credit what he wrote, then you think we have gone astray.* Although he is of the English race, who gave you such intelligence, yet, teacher, even as your wisdom teaches you, reason on this subject and believe only what is worthy of belief. O teacher, give great heed to this business. * * * Since the arrival of Moung Na Gau and Moung Tha Oung, and having heard from the teachers, I think much about returning with them.

* This has reference to an infidel foreigner, who wrote that the Christians had all turned back to their former religion, when, in fact, he was personally acquainted with but one of them, and knew nothing of their situation.

Although I am a young man, and have no wife, yet up to this time it has been more difficult for me to go to you, than for a married man. My father and mother have great age and cannot labor. It is very hard for me to leave my brother, Moung Too, alone, as he is not able to support them. When I reflect on our present situation, I have no desire for earthly happiness; neither do I desire afflictions; but if it was the will of God, I should be willing to leave this world. We have hope that this time of great distress and fear will not continue much longer. Our hope is in God."

After perusing this letter, Mr. Kincaid was led at once to direct his attention to another field of labor; and having carefully surveyed the ground, and finding it impossible to enjoy the facilities necessary to successful missionary work at either Maulmain or Rangoon, he at length decided to turn his face toward Arracan.

The remarkable and cheering results which there followed his devoted efforts, I shall attempt briefly to sketch in the succeeding chapter.

CHAPTER XIII.

A GREAT WORK IN ARRACAN.

"He shall come down like rain upon the mown grass; as showers that water the earth. They that dwell in the wilderness shall bow before him."

Ps. lxxii. 6, 9.

"Rich dews of grace come o'er us,
In many a gentle shower,
And brighter scenes before us
Are opening every hour."

WRITING from Maulmain, under date of January 20th, 1840, Mr. Kincaid gives the reasons which influenced him in deciding to go to Arracan. Prominent among these was that nothing worthy of being called missionary work could be accomplished. "Like the merchants," said he, "we could sit in our houses, and if this were all that was necessary, we could keep the ground. There is no difficulty about living in Burmah, but we could not teach the people, for the people dare not come near us." While this state of things existed, and there were other large fields open to our efforts, it seemed not the part of wisdom to remain in Burmah. The command is plain, "If they persecute you in one city, flee to another." These very circumstances, however, God was pleased to overrule for his own glory.

Paul, at one time, was forbid of the Spirit to preach the word in Asia, nor was he suffered to go into Bithynia, because, in the divine arrangement, he must first preach the gospel to a people made ready in Macedonia.

Judging from results, we might infer a similar purpose in the providences which compelled Mr. Kincaid to retire from Burmah, and led him to seek a temporary location in Arracan.

Fixing his residence at the city of Akyab, we find Mr. Kincaid, as in other instances, zealously prosecuting his work at all the points to which from this centre he could possibly gain access. And in these scattered fields he was soon permitted to witness some of the most wonderful displays of God's grace.

In a letter dated May 4th, 1840, he writes of his plans and prospects as follows:

"I preach three times on the Sabbath in my own house, and four times during the week in three different places in the town. My assemblies vary from twenty-two to twenty-three to more than one hundred hearers. Few come to the house, though every day from five or six to twenty. The heat is very great; the thermometer rarely falling below 90°, and much of the time during the day it is up to 95° and 97°, in the coolest part of the house. My two native assistants are every thing I can wish. They labor hard, and really try to win souls to Christ.

We have three hopeful inquirers. One is Moung Loon, a man about forty-five years old. He came in from the country after medical aid, and the first time he heard the gospel, it made a deep impression on his mind. Every day he comes and listens, and appears to have correct views of God and the way of life through Christ. I have no evidence, however, that he has yet felt the renovating power of the Holy Spirit, but his mind is rapidly passing from the delusions of heathenism to the clear light of the gospel. Another inquirer, is Moung Yau That, a young man seventeen or eighteen years old—his father and mother were baptized more than twenty years ago near Chittagong, and are the only consistent Christians in this little church. He appears to be truly awakened to a sense of his lost condition as a sinner. Ma Pong, a young woman, nineteen years old, is the wife of Moung Na Gau,—she listens with eagerness to the gospel, and gives us encouragement to hope that she is not far from the kingdom of heaven. There are three or four other persons who manifest more than usual interest in listening to the instruc tions of the word of God, but as yet they appear stupidly indifferent about the state of their own souls.

Between my own labors and those of the two assistants, from one to two hundred persons hear the gospel daily. Many dispute with an ingenuity and earnestness which might well put to shame idle and ease-loving ministers of Christ. It is often truly affecting to see the deep workings of the Spirit, and the anxiety, in mustering arguments to sustain that religion which they and their fathers have revered, and around which have centered all their fondest recollections and their most cherished hopes. All false religions will walk together in fellowship, but the uncompromising claims of the gospel, when they do not compel respect and attention, awaken the most bitter opposition. The heathen are accustomed to respect all religions, because, like civil institutions, they regard them as adapted to the various circumstances and wants of different nations. They are often pleased, therefore, with the gospel, at first, but when they come to understand its fearful denunciations against idolatry and all unrighteousness of men —that it pronounces the whole world in a state of apostacy from God—that all men without faith in Christ are without God, and have no hope, and in the end must everlastingly perish,—when they understand these things, and that the gospel is the only system of truth and the only refuge for the whole race of man, they either become patient hearers, or bitter opposers, or, as is sometimes the case, they take refuge in infidelity."

Among a number of inquirers who frequently called upon him, was one who awakened unusual interest, owing to his peculiar sentiments and high position in society. He was called M'ha-don, a title given him by the king of Ava, and may be regarded as furnishing rather a striking case of heathen transcendentalism :—

"He called on me," says Mr. Kincaid, "because I had lived in Ava, and from that time onward he appears to have felt a deep conviction that Budhism has more falsehood than truth. He has continued his visits and attended public worship. For many years past he has regarded outward Budhism—that is, prostrations and prayers and offerings before pagodas and idols—as adapted only to the ignorant, unthinking multitude ; and like many others of a contemplative turn of mind, had taken refuge in Pantheism, or the abstract, mystical doctrines of Budhism. All objects recognized by the senses are to be regarded as illusions, alike degrading to the mind and destructive of happiness ; and therefore, every thing which is pleaing, harmonious, and beautiful, is to be avoided, and the outward senses to be blunted and crushed, to the very utmost. The highest possible virtue, and so the most perfect happiness, is *indifference.* Praise and blame are alike ; nothing pleases, nothing offends ; nothing gratifies, nothing disgusts. You are neither to like nor dislike ; the mind is to be in a state of perfect equilibrium. Then all idea of one's self, or individual identity, is lost or absorbed in the divine essence, as a drop of water loses its form and individual character when cast into the ocean. Connection with matter, or material substance, therefore, is the cause of evil, and the gratification of the senses, is to commit sin. Neither the eye, nor ear, nor taste, nor feeling, should be gratified. Even conjugal, parental, and filial affection are only so many forms of selfishness. To own any thing which affords pleasure, or to which any relative value can be attached, is only to gratify *self*, or the individual being. While the highest efforts of virtue consist in rooting out all idea of self, or individual existence, and so bringing back the soul to an eternal, though unconscious repose."

One day, on the occasion of a baptism, this learned and venerable man was at the water, and united with them in singing two hymns, and afterwards paid the utmost attention to all that was said and done. When the converts came out of the water, in answer to a question which some one put to him, he replied in an earnest and elevated tone of voice, "This is the true religion, and I must be baptized and be a disciple of Christ." His constant attendance at worship created a great sensation all over the city. The priests had a meeting to inquire into the cause of his extraordinary conduct, and to them, in the most frank and open manner, he said—"I have found the true religion after worshiping idols and pagodas for more than ninety years."

Another case of peculiar interest was that of Moung Loon, a young man of great promise. The day following his baptism he came very early in the morning, saying that he had not slept during the entire night, and such a deep sense had he of the love of Christ in bearing in his own body the sins of men, that he could only pray and weep for joy.

About this time Mr. Kincaid was greatly encouraged by the intelligence which reached him of the wonderful triumphs of the gospel among the Karens of Bassein province. This great rejoicing had its beginning in the latter part of 1837, and its influence continued to spread from village to village until converts were counted by thousands:

"All the men," writes Mr. Kincaid in his journal, "who have come over the hills, represent the work as still going on; spreading from village to village, in every direction. Moung Shway Moung, who was baptized the latter part of 1835, was appointed by the king, governor of all the Karens in the Bassein province. He was sent down from Ava the latter part of 1837—the Karens soon found he was a disciple of Christ, and that he would shield them to the utmost of his power from oppression and persecution. The Karens testify that 'he was a just man, and would never take bribes,'—' that on the Sabbath he closed up his house, and remained alone.' About this time, the conversion of the celebrated young chief took place. He is a young man of great energy and powerful intellect, and all his influence was thrown into the work of publishing the knowledge of God among his countrymen. The full extent of this revival we do not know, but enough has been learned to convince us that it is an extraordinary display of divine grace. Probably more than *two thousand souls* are turned from the worship of demons to the service of the living God. This too has taken place under the jealous and intolerant reign of the new king. It is God's glorious work."

In the early spring of 1841, the lamented Comstock, with his family, made a visit to Akyab, and during a stay of about sixteen days joined Mr. Kincaid in an interesting preaching excursion. They visited a number of villages, and went as far as the old town of Arracan. Here they preached to large and solemn assemblies, both in private houses and in the open air. A few were found disposed to revile the truth, but the great mass would honestly acknowledge they were in the dark, and knew of no way to escape the pains and punishment of hell. "I have lived seventy years," said one, "and have labored to keep the five great commands, and have practised the austerities, but have not found peace." "The power and glory of our religion," said another, "has long been waning and must entirely vanish." Such impressions seemed to prevail at this time among the people. Some of the villagers who received tracts and heard the gospel during this excursion, soon afterwards came to Akyab, and were able to repeat much of what they had heard, saying also, that they had almost every evening read what had been given them, and having found in them *wonderful words*, they had come for more.

In the city of Akyab, many interesting cases of inquiry occurred. Among these was a man of great wealth and influence. He had for two or three years been making arrangements to build a large Kyoung (monastery) and had already expended many hundred rupees, when, for the first time, he heard the gospel. So affected was he by the truth that he dismissed his workmen, and resolved to let the building alone till he should examine fully the claims of the new religion.

Another very intelligent man, after being a diligent inquirer for several months, came saying that he had been proud of his ability to dispute, and had confided in his own wisdom, instead of receiving like a little child the word of God. This man after being driven from all the strongholds of Budhism, and acknowledging there was an eternal God, rejected the doctrine of substitution. Reformation, he thought, would secure the Divine favor, and especially if connected with sincere endeavors to keep the law. How it was possible for the suffering and death of Christ to satisfy the claims of justice on behalf of millions of the human race, he could not understand, and therefore the miraculous birth and deity of Christ he regarded as a fable, appended to the Christian religion. He was led to take this view of the subject by the Mohammedans, with whom he associated a good deal. His mind, however, was not at rest,—truth had taken too deep a hold of his conscience. One day Mr. Kincaid read and explained for several hours the first chapter of the epistle to the Hebrews. The next day he told Ko Bike that he had read and prayed nearly all night, and felt very unhappy, for he thought he was not to live long, and must certainly go to hell. In this state of feeling he remained for several days, when he came with a joyous countenance, and said he had obtained peace. "Now I know," he said, "what it is to believe in Christ, for I have the evidence in my own heart."

It is characteristic of the Burmans frequently to interrupt those who are preaching, for the purpose of asking questions; and an instance or two of this kind, as recorded in Mr. Kincaid's journal, may serve to give a general idea of what is sometimes witnessed under such circumstances:

"By the request of a respectable man," he writes

"I went to preach in his house, but the heat was suffocating, and we went into the street, where mats were spread for the people, and a chair brought for me. The moon shone brilliantly, so that I could read the large Burman characters with ease. After preaching about thirty minutes, so many questions were asked, that it was quite impossible to pursue my subject further. Questions, however absurd, must be answered, and if they are not proposed too often, are useful in fixing the attention of the people. This evening I was overwhelmed. Many persons, however, remained silent and attentive, and perhaps have not heard in vain.

In the evening I preached in the same place to a still larger assembly, and with less interruption. When I closed the book, one man took up manfully on the side of Gaudama, and a discussion for nearly two hours followed. One man who had been a great opposer, occasionally threw in a word to confirm the statements I made, and as he was a man of acknowledged ability in explaining the legends of Gaudama, my adversary forsook the sober field of argument, and began to ridicule and revile this heretic, as he called him. 'You have become a disciple of Christ, have you? You join with this foreign teacher, do you, to prove that our god is no god, and that our religion, which has stood a thousand years, is only a cheat and a fable? Who will carry you to the grave when you die? Your own father and mother will despise you, and your brothers and sisters will shun you as they would a leper. You are like a dog that is coaxed away by a thief—you may as well lick honey from the edge of a razor as to listen to this foreigner.' 'Very well,' replied my new ally, 'I have reviled this religion and this teacher more than you have, but I was a fool with both my eyes shut—his religion is true, and everybody would believe it if they knew what it is. We make a god of wood, and then put a rope round his neck, and carry him off to his own place, and then put a fence around him, and keep him there till the white ants eat him up. We would not serve a thief as bad as this. There is as much evidence to prove that Gaudama was a monkey, as that he was a god.' Some of the people with rage at this bold assertion from one of their own learned men, put their fingers in their ears and went away—but still a large number listened to the very last. It was eleven o'clock at night."

But the most interesting occurrence, perhaps, that marked the history of Mr. Kincaid's connection with the Akyab Station, was the visit of Chet-za, the "mountain chief." His first interview with this man took place in the month of May, 1841. Early in July following, he received from him a very interesting and earnest letter, in which, after giving his own name and title, "Chet-za, the great mountain chief," he added the names of thirteen petty chiefs, who were his neighbors, and then went on to state that they and their people for ages have been without the knowledge of God and his law—that they have no books, and, therefore, can neither read nor write —that in ancient days, God gave their fathers a good book, written on leather, but being careless, a dog carried it away and destroyed it, and thus the divine displeasure appeared against them—that they are anxious to know the true God, and be taught the true book, though no one has ever appeared till now, "bringing the *good book.*" "Our sons and our daughters we shall deliver over to you to be taught, if you will have compassion on us." Then followed a list of two hundred and seventy-three names of boys and girls whom they wished to place in school, if the teacher would come to their mountains.

"There is," writes Mr. Kincaid, "something singular, as well as deeply interesting, in this request. From time immemorial they have had intercourse with Burmans, but have resisted idolatry. They have looked with apathy, if not with contempt, upon the imposing ceremonies of Budhism—its temples, pagodas, monasteries, idols, shaven-headed priests, its ten thousand burning tapers, its prostrations, its beads, its celebrated shrines, and its pilgrimages. Like the Karens in Tenasserim, and in Burmah, they appear to be looking for the '*good book*' which will tell them of the true God. There is an overruling Providence in this, and the request of the Mountain Chief and his friends, sounds to me like the Macedonian cry, 'Come over and help us.'"

CHAPTER XIV.

VISIT TO THE MOUNTAIN CHIEF.

"The mountains and the hills shall break forth before you into singing."
Isa. lv. 12.

"The dwellers in the vales and on the rocks
Shout to each other, and the mountain tops,
From distant mountains, catch the flying joy."

TOWARD the close of the year 1841, and just as Mr. Kincaid had perfected his arrangements for a visit to the mountains, Chet-za, fearing he was to be disappointed in his hopes, made another visit to Akyab, urging him to come at once, and teach his people the true religion. Accordingly, on the 29th of December, accompanied by the Rev. L. Stilson, he set out on his interesting tour.

The graphic account given by him of the journey, of the population, and of their reception among that remarkable people, will be found replete with interest:—

"We crossed the spacious harbor," says Mr. Kincaid, "and entered the Ko-la-dan, a broad and noble river which has its sources in the Yuma mountains far to the north. After ascending the Ko-la-dan between seventy and eighty miles, we left all Burman population, and entered the Kemmee country. The change in the scenery is not less striking than the change in the character, habits, and manners of the people. For the last seventy miles before it empties its waters into the Akyab harbor, the Ko-la-dan flows through a vast tract of level plain, dotted with villages in every direction. Rice fields are extensive,—in many places as far as the eye can reach. Here and there are dark tangled forests. There are no fences, no hedges. Occasionally we see small patches of tobacco, and a few gourds and plantains, and besides this there is no cultivation, although the soil is exceedingly rich, and capable of producing every kind of plant and vegetable peculiar to warm latitudes.— The delta for twenty-five or thirty miles inland is intersected by innumerable creeks, lined with various kinds of mangroves, which give the country a sombre aspect; and is a great laboratory of the most deadly fevers. When about thirty miles from the sea there is a slight elevation of the land, and mountains appear in the distance, but still there is little change in the aspect of the country. When we leave the plains we leave also the Burman, or as they are called in Arracan, the *Mug* population. First we came to low ranges of hills, but every ten miles we ascended, the hills became larger and were clothed with dark tangled forests to the very summit. The river is still broad and deep—it makes a few curves, but its general course is exactly from north to south. As we were anxious to reach the village where the chief lives, with as little delay as possible, we visited only one of the numerous Kemmee villages along the river. It was about ten in the morning; the boatmen were cooking their rice on the bank of the river—the forest came down to the very water's edge, and the only indication of their being a village at hand, was a small landing-place up the steep bank. Mr. Stilson and I found a path, and after walking about four or five hundred yards, came to a village of seventeen houses, surrounded by a neat and well constructed stockade. The gate was open and we went in, but saw no human being. After standing a few minutes in order to give no unnecessary alarm, and admiring the peculiar structure of their great houses,—the neat and orderly manner in which they were placed,—that is, in two rows, so as to have a broad street running through the centre,—we passed on, and finally went out at the gate on the opposite end of the village, and found ourselves standing on the bank of a noisy little brook—an object of great interest to us, as it was the first of the kind we had seen in Arracan. We saw abundance of pigs, goats and fowls, and began to wonder where the inhabitants could be, as we saw none and did not hear a human voice. We suspected, what in the end turned out to be true, that the men were in their fields at a distance, while the females and children, ascertaining that extraordinary looking strangers were at the landing, had fled in a panic to the jungles. We were sorry to alarm them, but still did not feel willing to go away till we could see them, and give them every assurance that we were friends. While examining two or three peculiar trees which grew on the margin of the brook, a female with a child slung on her back, rose up out of the grass but a few feet from us. She appeared to be paralyzed with fear, and the poor little urchin on her back was afraid to look up. We could not help reflecting on the wrong and outrage which have induced such a feeling of dread at the appearance of strangers—more terrifying than the midnight growl of the most ferocious beasts of prey. We stepped back and spoke soothingly to the poor woman, assured her, again and again, that she had nothing to fear; and she evidently believed us, for in a little time she went into the village. Probably on the first alarm one or more had been despatched to give intelligence to the men, for they soon began to come in, and then the females came from their hiding places, each one with a child slung on her back, and many of them with three or four or half a dozen older children following them. The men came and sat down around us, while the females and children remained at a distance, or went up into their houses. Some of the men could understand Burman, and speak it tolerably well. We soon perceived, however, that they could not sound the final consonant, or the *th*, to which they always gave the sound of *s*. We explained to them our design in coming into their country—that it was in obedience to the command of God, to visit all nations and instruct them in his holy word. They appeared to be much interested ; said they should be glad to have books, and understand those things of which we told them. After returning to our boat, several of the men came down and wished us to accept of a fowl which they brought.

The next day, in the morning, we came to the mouth of the river *Moe*, a fine stream which comes in from the north-east, and is from fifty to sixty yards broad. Up this river about six miles, we came to the village where the Mountain Chief resides. This village is situated in a large bend in the river, on a fine elevation, one hundred feet above the present level of the water, and commands a beautiful prospect in this wild and picturesque country. Three other villages are in sight, and the fourth is not a mile distant. There is apparently but little level ground, it being a perfect contrast to all we had seen for seventy miles above Akyab. Here are lofty hills and deep vallies, and all thrown together in the utmost confusion. The hills as well as vallies are covered with tall forest trees, interspersed with bamboos, various kinds of creepers, and occasionally with a coarse grass that grows from ten to twelve feet high.

From the anxiety which the chief had manifested to have us visit him and his people, we had every reason to expect a kind reception. For the last eight or ten months it had been his constantly expressed wish to have us establish schools among them, and teach them the knowledge of God, but still we had not anticipated so much attention, or rather, so much forethought in reference to our comfort. To our surprise we found a new and well constructed zayat about fifty feet above the present level of the river, sixteen feet by twenty-one, and the ground cleared away so as to make a pleasant walk, and a verandah on one side. But what surprised us most, was two very neat bamboo bedsteads, surrounded with curtains. The chief must have seen a bedstead in our house at Akyab, and so got the idea that this was our manner of sleeping. He returned only four or five days before we left, and during two of these days, there was a very severe storm of wind and rain, which made us wonder how he could possibly have put up such a building. On inquiring of him, he said the whole, from the foundation to the roof, including bedsteads and all, were made in two days.

Visit to the Mountain Chief.

When he saw we had a small folding-table and two chairs, he felt greatly relieved, for he had felt very sad, he said, to think he could construct no such articles for us. I mention these facts to shew the kind-heartedness of the chief and his people, and their anxiety to make us comfortable. Our zayat was about fifty yards from the stockade which surrounded the village, and in a delightful situation. After getting everything arranged in our new home and ready to begin work, we went up into the village and were taken directly to the house of the Mountain Chief (as he is called). It is certainly no mean specimen of a palace, for though constructed on the same general plan with all the houses of this peculiar people, yet its dimensions and neatness of construction would point it out as the residence of a great man. Like all the houses, the floor is between five and six feet from the ground. After passing across a very large open verandah, we entered, immediately in front, the great hall of audience. It is certainly a fine room, and from the north end we have a most delightful view of the country in all the wildness of its native grandeur. We spent some time in conversation, but most of the time in getting words and sentences expressed in their own language. I left the company at length, and went to take a view of the domestic arrangements. On the left of the great verandah is a very large apartment, and on the right is one of smaller dimensions ; these belong to the females and children. His wives—nine in number—were all busily at work, except one. Some were cleaning cotton, some spinning, some weaving and some were cooking ; and each one had a child slung on her back, whatever the work might be in which she was engaged. All appeared to be cheerful. It was easy to perceive that the female who was not at work, was a person of no ordinary rank among this people. There was a gracefulness and dignity in her manners which could not fail to impress the most casual observer that she was one of "nature's noble women." Her countenance is intelligent, and her features would indicate a mild and amiable temper. Her face was covered with smiles, so that she appeared to be pleased with herself and pleased with all around her. She was the only one of the females who appeared to have any knowledge of the Burman language, and hers, I imagine, is very limited, for though she betrayed in her countenance no signs of ignorance, yet she was able to reply to me only in a few half-formed sentences. We were struck with the order and neatness of the apartments. There were no articles lying about the floor, as is always the case in Burman houses, whatever may be their rank. True, there was no furniture for mere show, and little which we regard as necessary to comfort in civilized life ; still they have many articles for the manufacture of cloth, for cooking, for holding water, and for eating, and though they be of the most primitive kind, they all had their appropriate place. The internal arrangements of the apartments and the furniture, no less than the neat and comfortable manner in which the houses are constructed, as well as the orderly arrangement of the whole village, certainly struck us as indicating, in a more than ordinary degree, an innate sense of neatness and regularity. The posts which supported the roof are formed by binding together ten or twelve bamboos, so that at first they might be taken for fluted columns. The roofs of the houses are made of long coarse grass. The walls are double ; the outer extending from the ground to the roof, and the inner from the floor to the roof. The outer wall is formed by placing perfectly straight bamboos, and all of the same size, horizontally one on top of the other, till they reach the top ; these are kept together by upright posts at suitable distances. This wall gives the house a very substantial and pretty appearance. The inner wall is made of split bamboos woven into mats. The stairs for going up into their houses are of the same material, and are broad and well formed, while the people of Arracan have only a large pole, with notches cut in it. In fact, everything pertaining to the houses and villages of the Kemmees indicates an attention to comfort which we have seen among no other class of people in these countries.

Their clothing is scanty and peculiar. Besides a small turban on the head, the only garment ordinarily worn by the men is a belt about *four* inches wide, fastened round the hips and between the legs ; one end of the belt hanging down before, and one behind. The females have two garments—the upper, a short jacket about ten or twelve inches long, without sleeves and open under one arm ; the lower garment is fastened round the hips and reaches half way to the knees. It is remarkable that a people who consult neatness and comfort to so great a degree in the construction of their villages and houses, should have adopted so scanty a covering for their persons. It cannot be for want of *material*, for they grow a fine, beautiful species of cotton on their hills, and in exchange for cotton procure salt and dried fish from the coast. * * *

For some wise purpose God has preserved them from idolatry, and kept alive among them the tradition, that in ancient times the Supreme Being gave to their fathers a *Good Book*, which through their carelessness was destroyed by a dog, but which in time will be restored, when they will become a wise and happy people. We preached the gospel every evening in the most plain and simple manner, and they listened attentively ; but few could understand

Burman well enough to receive much instruction. Those who could understand, said they believed what we taught, and that all the Kemmees would believe when they came to hear and understand this doctrine. From morning till night we spent nearly all our time in collecting words and sentences so as to learn the structure of the language, but still embraced every opportunity to learn the extent of their country and the probable number of the inhabitants. All we could learn, however, on this last subject was, that for several days' journey (two hundred miles or more,) up the great river, and on all the tributary streams, the inhabitants are Kemmees. The Ko-la-dan, and all its tributaries, are thickly studded with their villages, which vary from ten to fifty families in each. They are certainly a numerous people, and, without doubt, I think, one of the greatest branches of the Karen family. The Khyiens inhabit all the hill country and the great ranges of the Yuma mountains to the south, as the Kemmees do at the north. After getting about eighty miles north of Ava, I found all the hill country for more than three hundred miles, that is, to the Hu Kong valley, inhabited by Ka Khyiens, a people in all respects like the Karens; so that we have Karens, Ka Khyiens, Khyiens and Kemmees, four branches of the same great family, formerly the sole occupants of this vast country, but who have been gradually driven by the Burmans from the valley of the Irrawaddy and from the sea-coast. On the fourth day after our arrival at the village of the chief, the path of duty appeared to be plain. We accordingly intimated to him, and some of his people, that we should study the language, adopt an alphabet, and as soon as possible give them books in which they could learn the knowledge of God. As might have been expected, they were greatly pleased. In a short time word was brought to us that the chief was going into the neighboring villages to call together the principal men, and would immediately commence building us a large house. We were obliged to hold him back, or the house would have been begun that very day. We told him we must return home and make arrangements for this work, for it was not a small thing to study their language and get ready to give them books; however, they might expect Mr. Stilson and his family in about twenty days, and that I should, probably, be up again in a month after that. We selected a place for building, and told the chief he might collect the materials at his leisure, that on Mr. Stilson's arrival a house could be put up in a few days. He told Ko Bike that our decision gave him more joy than if he had received thousands of gold and silver, for, said he, 'The gold and silver would soon be expended, and neither my children nor my people would be any the better for it; but if we have the knowledge of God, I shall die in peace.'

This indicates a degree of intelligence and earnestness which we did not expect to find, and which goes far to encourage us that it is the Lord's work. This village, which we have resolved to make the head-quarters of the Kemmee mission, possesses all the advantages we could desire,—its location is beautiful and healthy,—it is not too far in the interior, and still is far enough to be the centre of a number of villages, embracing, at least, about three thousand inhabitants. It is two degrees north of Akyab, and, therefore, distant on a straight line, one hundred and thirty-eight miles. There are a few curves in the river, so that the distance, by water, is one hundred and fifty miles. Mr. Stilson took the latitude of the village, and made it 22° 3′ north, which would make it twelve or thirteen miles north of Ava. No foreigner has ever been up the river beyond the boundaries of Arracan, and Burmans are afraid to penetrate; so that the extent of the Kemmee country north, can only be conjectured from the statements of the Kemmees themselves. They speak of two powerful bodies of people far to the north, called Lung-khe, and Tsein-du, who differ somewhat from them in language. I would remark here, that Kemmee is the generic name of this people, though they have a great number of local names. This extraor dinary variety of names for one and the same people, originates partly from location and partly from clanship; in some cases, the name of a stream gives a name to the people; and, in other cases, the name of a chief to whose authority they submit. Our intercourse with the Kemmees has been too limited to say much in reference to their national manners and customs,—their vices and their virtues. Polygamy, I should think, does not prevail to any great extent. They have learnt how to make an intoxicating drink from rice, which is used on extraordinary occasions. They regard evil spirits as the principal cause of disease, as also of all other calamities, when they cannot trace them to human agency. This belief in evil demons leads them to offer, on certain occasions, propitiatory sacrifices. They have no religious services, though they believe in a Supreme Being,—in the immortality of the soul, and in future rewards and punishments. Murder, adultery, stealing, and falsehood, are regarded as great crimes, and there is much reason to suppose that these are not their national vices. They are, proverbially, a people of *one word.*

It is very possible that many might get the impression, from the preceding remarks, that the Kemmees are a harmless, unwarlike people, but such is not the case. Broken up, as they are, into clans under different chiefs, who are supreme among their own people, serious difficulties are rarely, if ever, adjusted in an amicable manner. Feuds are frequent, and often end most disastrously. When one clan nourishes revenge or hatred against another, from whatever cause, an opportunity is sought to fall upon their enemies at a time when least expected. An open declaration of hostile intentions is never made. The triumphant party kill as many men as they can, and all the females and children they can seize are carried away for slaves. Those clans located within the limits of Arracan, are, of course, subject to British rule, and they appear to appreciate the advantages of living in a state of security under the protection of law. Depending for their subsistence almost entirely on the cultivation of the soil, war is not the natural element of the Kemmees; it is rather a circumstance growing out of their peculiar condition.

The introduction of books, and the establishment of schools, will lay the foundation of their civilization and happiness, because the first lessons they learn, will be the knowledge of God. This knowledge will spread over the whole length and breadth of the land, and convert this wilderness into a fruitful field."

Subsequently Mr. Kincaid made several visits to this people, and Mr. Stilson, in the course of a brief residence, studied their language, and having reduced its elements to writing, was the means of supplying them with a number of books. At a still later period, they were visited by Mr. Ingalls, whose labors among them, under the divine blessing, resulted in a number of hopeful conversions. Among those baptized was Paiting, son of the Mountain Chief, a young man of marked piety, who often, in his private devotions, would be heard pleading with God for his countrymen, and in every prayer his fervent cry was—"Oh, Lord, send a teacher from America for the Kemmees."

CHAPTER XV.

VISIT TO AMERICA.

"For not he that commendeth himself is approved, but whom the Lord commendeth."--2 Cor. x. 18.

"The man of God, O give him welcome home!
For many long and weary years he's roamed;
And now, once more, he hails his native land;—
O give him greetings warm, a brother's hand."

MR. KINCAID had now been in Burmah more than twelve years, and the health of his wife requiring a change of climate, it was determined that he should make a visit to his native land, which he did in 1833.

The reception which he here met, afforded striking proof of the hold which he had upon the hearts of his brethren, and the results which followed his efforts to awaken a missionary spirit in the churches, were regarded as quite astonishing. During his sojourn in this country he traveled through nearly every State in the Union, making his thrilling appeals to the people, and awakening, every where, a new and marvelous interest in behalf of foreign missions.

To follow him through all the remarkable incidents connected with this visit, is more than I am prepared to attempt, nor will the limits of a single chapter allow of any thing beyond a brief reference to a few of the leading features of this memorable period in his history.

The character and influence of his public addresses may, to a degree, be inferred from reports which, in some instances, were attempted to be made for the press, and yet to those who have never heard him, these must necessarily convey a very imperfect idea of their effect as they fell directly from his own lips. To appreciate them fully, the reader must have before his mind the person of the speaker; he must be able to call up his peculiar intonations, but especially must he remember his lofty and impassioned strain of utterance when, all aglow with his subject, every fibre of his frame appeared to tremble with emotion, and every sensibility of his soul seemed stirred to its depths and roused to its intensest activity.

Never, while memory remains, can any forget the impression made on the heart in listening to the account given by him of the parting interview of the lamented COMSTOCK'S with their two children, and of the last words Mr. Comstock uttered to Mr. Kincaid. Owing to the difficulty of educating them in a heathen land, they were entrusted to Mr. Kincaid's care, to be taken to America, and the following extract from one of his addresses gives an affecting view of their painful separation :—

"We were together one day, at their house, when word came that the ship was ready to sail, and we must prepare to embark immediately. Upon the arrival of this message, which we had been expecting, Mrs. Comstock arose from her seat, took her two children, one in each hand, and walked with them towards a grove of tamarind trees near the house. When she had walked some little distance, she paused a moment, looked at each of her children with all a mother's love, and imprinted an affectionate kiss upon the forehead of each. She then raised her eyes to heaven, silently invoked a blessing on their heads; returned to the house, and delivering her children into my hands, said, 'Brother Kincaid, *this I do for my Saviour.*'

Brother Comstock then took his two children by the hand, and led them from the house towards the ship, while that tender mother gazed upon them. as they walked away, *for the last time.* She saw them no more on earth. God grant that she may meet them in heaven! Brother Comstock accompanied his two children to the ship, which lay about two miles off in the bay. When we had descended to the cabin, he entered one of the state-rooms with his children. There he knelt with them in prayer, laid his hands upon their heads, and bestowed a father's blessing upon them—the tears, all the while, streaming down his cheeks. This affecting duty over, he resumed, at once, his usual calmness. He took leave of me with a gentle pressure of the hand, and I followed him to the side of the vessel, as he descended into the small boat which lay along-side, and which was to convey him to the shore. Never shall I forget the words, or the tone in which those words were uttered, as he turned up his face, still bedewed with tears, and exclaimed, as the boat moved away, 'REMEMBER, BROTHER KINCAID, SIX MEN FOR ARRACAN!'

I never saw brother or sister Comstock after that. The very day that we took a pilot on board off Sandy Hook, April 28th, 1843, was the day that sister Comstock died, and in one year afterward, lacking three days, that is, on the 25th of April, 1844, brother Comstock followed her. Now they sleep side by side in the grave-yard at Ramree, under the tamarind trees; and sister Abbott and her children are buried in the same ground.

Ah, my Christian friends, could you have witnessed the parting of these beloved missionaries with their children;—could you have stood with the survivors by the graves of the loved ones who lie buried on those heathen shores, you would then have known something of what it is to make sacrifices for the missionary cause.

Once more let me call upon this audience to remember the last parting words of the beloved Comstock! and then let me ask, in the name of my departed brother, and of Jesus, the Master whom he served—shall we go back to that heathen land without 'SIX MEN FOR ARRACAN?'"

It was this noble illustration of Christian heroism, so touchingly related, that called from the pen of Charles Thurber, Esq., the following beautiful lines:

SIX MEN FOR ARRACAN.

THE mother stamp'd a burning kiss
Upon each little brow;
So dear a sacrifice as this,
She never made till now;
Go, go, my babes, the Sabbath bell
Will greet ye o'er the sea;
I'll bid my idol ones farewell,
For Thee, my God, for Thee.
But off they'd gone—those little ones—
I saw them gaily trip,
And chatter on in merry tones,
To see the gallant ship.
The stricken sire—he'd often drank
Sad draughts at duty's beck—
He leads them calmly o'er the plank,
And stands upon the deck;
As pale as polished Parian stones,
As white as Arctic snows,
Beside those young and cherished ones
The stricken father bows·
He breathes one prayer—he prints one kiss,
And turns him toward the shore—

He felt, till now, the babes were his,
But they were his no more;
The silken tie, more strong than death,
That bound their hearts was riven,
And floating on an angel's breath,
Rose up and clung to heaven.

Why lingers he upon the shore?
Why turns he to the deck?
Perhaps, to say farewell, once more,
Perhaps, one look to take.
O! no; but calm as angels now,
That kneel before the throne,
Where twice ten thousand thousand bow,
And say, "Thy will be done"
He said—"My brother, when you stand,
Beyond the raging deep,
In that delightful, happy land,
Where all our fathers sleep,
When you shall hear their Sabbath bell
Call out their happy throngs,
And hear the organ's solemn swell,
And Zion's sacred songs—
Tell them a herald, far away,
Where midnight broods o'er man,
Bade ye this solemn message say,
"Six men for Arracan."

While in that happy land of theirs,
They feast on blessings given,
And genial suns and healthful airs,
Come speeding fresh from heaven;
Tell them, that, near yon idol dome,
There dwells a lonely man,
Who bade ye take this message home,
"*Six men for Arracan.*

Sweet home—ah, yes! I know how sweet
Within my country, thou,
I've known what heart-felt pleasures meet—
I've felt—and feel them now.
Well, in those lively scenes of bliss,
Where childhood's joys began,
I'd have ye, brother, tell them this,
"SIX MEN FOR ARRACAN."

O! when the saint lies down to die.
And friendship round him stands,
And faith directs his tearless eye,
To fairer, happier lands—
How calm he bids poor earth adieu!
With all most dear below!
The spirit sees sweet home in view,
And plumes her wings to go.
Stop, dying saint—O! linger yet,
And cast one thought on man—
Be this the last that you forget—
"SIX MEN FOR ARRACAN."

In the month of November, 1843, a number of missionary meetings, remarkable for their interest and results, were held with the various Baptist churches in Philadelphia. At one of these gatherings, in the large round house of the Sansom-St. Church, after the reading of an able report by the Rev. Dr. Williams, on the Duty of Churches in reference to the Mission Cause, Mr. Kincaid rose to move its adoption. "There are a great many intelligent people," said he, "who have seriously made it a question, whether we, in this day, are to expect the same success as marked the history of primitive Christians, in their efforts to furnish the heathen with the precious Gospel.

My brethren, if I had never read a single missionary letter, if I had read nothing but the acts of the Apostles, I feel well satisfied, that if we preach the Gospel in all its length and breadth, and richness, and in the same spirit and labor to win souls as did the primitive Christians, we should have in some degree the same success. If at present, we do not meet with the same or like success, the reason is, that we do not preach in the same spirit, and have not the same love for souls as they had. I would inquire whether we have not had success; and would reply, look to our brethren on missionary ground, and look at the results of their labors, and we have great reason to take courage. Why, just as we are beginning to think about doing this great work, the windows of heaven are opened, and a blessing is poured down upon us.

In 1830, how many missionaries had we in Burmah?—only three, and of these only two were qualified to preach the Gospel. Brother Bennet was engaged in printing, while brethren Wade and Boardman had only been a short time able to preach in their language. It took two years before either of them could be prepared for preaching in Burmese. It was not until 1834, that the missionaries were reinforced ; and from that time down to 1836, and to the present time, we have only had about seven or eight men actually employed in preaching ; but much work has been done besides preaching the Gospel. The Bible has been translated, a dictionary and grammar prepared, tracts have been written and printed, and widely circulated, and the Karen language has been formed and reduced to writing ; and now the New Testament has been nearly translated in the Karen language, a hymn-book containing about five hundred hymns, also a grammar. Now the accomplishment of all this important work, devolved on the missionaries, so that there had not been more than seven missionaries at any one time engaged in preaching the Gospel, and yet our labors have been blessed.

* * * * * *

In looking, therefore, at these facts, we may truly say, that our preaching has not been in vain, and yet our missionary brethren all complain of want of faith in preaching to these poor idolators, and they are striving for more of the faith of Paul and Barnabas ; now, when we can come up to the faith which they possessed, we shall no doubt experience more, and still greater, even, like success with them ; and, I think, the native preachers are rapidly arriving at this state of feeling. There was one native convert who fully believed—indeed, his faith was so strong, that he had no doubt that Jesus Christ came into the world to save the lost. and that all who sat under his preaching would be saved. This was, indeed, a wonderful instance of saving grace. He was a man taken from among the very lowest orders. I cannot tell of the bloody scenes he passed through. He became a robber, and a robber in Burmah is always a murderer, —and he was, therefore, a murderer. Indeed, I cannot tell of his wicked deeds. This brother, whose name was *Ko-tha-bu*, was a robber from his early life. Robbers in Burmah are men, who profess to execute the most horrid deeds. Their very countenances look as if all the feeling and compassion they ever enjoyed had been blotted out, and every trace of humanity lost in their character. This man, I say, whose muscular arm had never trembled, when with his drawn sword he stood over his victim—this man, whose lips had never quivered as he looked upon his slaughtered enemy—this man, whose eyes had never filled and overflowed with the tear of sympathy and compassion—this murderer, who, from early life up to the period of his conversion, had had his hands imbrued in the blood of his fellow-man—was, in the providence of God, separated from his wicked companions, and became a humble disciple of Christ. He heard the Gospel from the lips of a native preacher, and it reached his guilty soul, and he was brought by the power of God to submit to the cross of Christ, and there his heart was softened—that heart which could not weep over deeds of blood, wept over the cross of Christ. But it was a long time before the brethren could place confidence in his professions of attachment to the Saviour ; they could hardly realize that the change was real. Judson was afraid of him, and would not baptize him ; and Wade felt afraid of his connecting himself with the church ; but finally, Boardman had resolved upon going to Tavoy to proclaim the Gospel, and it was a new field, and he could not obtain the consent of any of his converts to accompany him, they were afraid to go. At length *Ko-tha-bu* came forward, and offered to go with him, and rather than go alone, Boardman consented to take him, as he had a little hope that the truth was in him. On their way, he frequently conversed with him on the subject of religion, and he saw so much of the spirit of Christ in him, that he was induced to baptize him, at the same time he feared lest he should baptize an unconverted man and not a Christian. After this, *Ko-tha-bu* insisted upon going to the hill country of Tavoy, to carry the Gospel to his countrymen, and when he returned, he brought with him thirty of these poor Karens, who had accompanied him in order to see the foreign teacher. The memory of the Karens is very tenacious ; they remember almost everything they hear, having to depend on their memory, as they have had no written language nor any books, until very lately. Ko-tha-bu preached daily to them Jesus and him crucified, and they remembered all he said; and when Boardman saw them he was surprised and delighted with their conversation, and at their knowledge of divine things, for it was wonderful in his eyes, and he talked with them and was satisfied that they were the children of God; but he was too weak to baptize them. In a very short time Br. Mason, who had just arrived in the country, visited Tavoy, and Boardman got him to baptize these Karen converts; and he was carried to the bank of the river, and being too ill to sit up, he was supported in the arms of Mrs. Boardman while he witnessed the sight.

But the labors of Ko-tha-bu did not stop here; he went on and preached Christ to his heathen countrymen. In 1835, brother Abbott and myself designed going to Arracan, and who should we get to accompany us? At last we obtained two Burmese and two Karens, one of whom was Ko-tha-bu, who, on being asked to go with us about seven hundred miles, made no objection. He seemed willing to go any where, so that he might impart the blessings of the gospel to his countrymen. He went with us; and in less than ten days after reaching the province, he was off searching out the villages, and going from house to house, preaching the word. But in about one year after this, he died there; not, however, until he had been instrumental in giving the gospel to more than three hundred. Now it may be said, that from first to last this man was compelled by an overpowering conviction that he must carry the gospel to all, and he seemed to have the impression that wherever he preached, converts would be made and churches would be organized. I was with this man enough to see and to testify to his spirit. He was naturally one of the most unamiable of men ; but by the subduing power of grace, he ruled over his own spirit : he had a burning love for souls, and that gospel which he preached, he believed sufficient to save all. I have been with him in the mountains, in cities, and on the plains. I have heard him pray in the congregation and in families, and I have overheard him in secret; and invariably, whenever and wherever he would engage, he would commence his prayer with a confession to God that he had been a great murderer ; and the big tear would roll down his cheeks, and his language was that of a penitent seeking forgiveness. Now who, in looking upon this instance, can doubt the power of God in Burmah! In this, as in other instances, God has shown us that the gospel has lost none of its power, and all that is wanted, is to carry the gospel believingly, and come with it to their villages and cottages—and their very doors—and publicly preach it, and God will bless it. * * * *

When I was about to leave India, I wrote brother Mason, and asked what I should get for him in America. His answer is, 'among all other things, remember, first, good preachers for Burmah; revivalist preachers—men who like nothing better than preaching and praying;' and then he breaks out and says —'Oh! America! with all thy treasures, there is nothing I wish but some of your men who are prepared of God for pentecostal seasons;' and as yet, not a single man has offered to go to the Mountain Chief, or to the other opening fields of labor. Now, I wonder whether, in the days of Paul, when the churches were small and few, whether there would not have been dozens to have said, 'Here am I—send me,' if a call like the present had reached them. It does appear to me, my brethren, that we have not begun to look at this subject as we should, to make it our duty morning and night, to pray over it, until the heart of every pastor and every church member is deeply imbued with the spirit of missions."

Being present at the special meeting of the Baptist General Convention, held in New York city, in the month of November, 1845, Mr. Kincaid was called upon during one of its sessions to speak. Dr. Judson, in his powerful plea for Arracan, had already awakened in the minds of the assembly an extraordinary degree of interest; but, notwithstanding this, the words of Mr. Kincaid contributed, if possible, to carry the feelings of the meeting tc a still higher pitch of excitement:—

"I bless God," said he, "for this day and the days that are past. I have never supposed for a single moment that one of our missions would be abandoned. So far as my experience goes—though that is but very limited, being confined to the Burman and Karen missions—but so far as it goes, no missionary in that great and idolatrous empire has ever labored for any considerable time, in any single place, without seeing the gospel take root in that heathen land. In every single place where they have gone and preached for any length of time, they have seen churches raised up there.

I never understood, as I now understand, a great many portions of the Holy Scriptures. 'Ask of me my Son, and I shall give thee the heathen for thine inheritance.' I recollect the very first time I landed on the shores of Burmah. It was about one o'clock at night, on the wharves of Rangoon. Brother Mason and I came up the Salwen River in Burman boats. A large crowd thronged around us, and among them were brethren Bennett and Wade. They welcomed us, but the natives with smiling faces thronged round us, and reached out their hands, almost every one of them uttering words as rapidly as possible. I asked, 'What do they say?' 'They are saying,' replied one of the brethren, 'welcome, welcome to this land.' This was on a Saturday night about one o'clock.

The next morning I heard Brother Wade preach,

and in the evening these native converts held a prayer meeting. Some fourteen or fifteen, almost every one of whom I could name, prayed one after the other. In their prayers I heard one word which was familiar to my ears, it was '*America, America.*' Every one of them, in their prayers pouring out their full hearts before God, had something to say about America. After the prayer meeting was over, I asked, 'What is it that they were all praying for about America?' and Mr. Wade's reply was, 'They were blessing God that their brethren in the great country of America had remembered them, and had sent out two more teachers to bring the gospel to their countrymen, and praying that the blessing of the Most High might rest upon those brethren and sisters in America.' Well, I said to myself, this is what God means. 'I will give thee the heathen for thine inheritance, and the uttermost parts of the earth for thy possession.' From that day forward I felt as I had never felt before. Long had my heart been set on carrying the gospel to the heathen, but after that day, I seemed to live by sight and not by faith."

The great object of Mr. Kincaid in all his journeyings and labors in different parts of the land, was to awaken in the churches a deeper interest and more enlarged liberality in behalf of the work of missions. This pressed constantly upon his mind,—to promote it he felt was his peculiar work, and he would not rest until he saw it, in a measure, accomplished:

"It is time," said he, writing from Kentucky to the late Dr. Cone, "to awake as we never have before, that the reapers may overtake them that sow, and gather in the precious harvest. More men must go to Arracan, and one more to Mergui. The seed sown is taking root and thousands are turning to God. It cannot be that the churches will slumber over these clear indications of divine providence, to go up and possess the land."

Nor was he mistaken in this opinion; for the churches *did* begin, in a measure, to awake to their responsibility, and throughout the country, but especially in the large cities, a liberality was exhibited in behalf of foreign missions surpassing any thing that had ever before been known in the history of American Baptists.

In addition to the efficient efforts of Mr. Kincaid to enlighten the churches with reference to the real state of the heathen, and to impress upon them their duty to the missionary enterprise, he was, also, chiefly instrumental in starting the new University of Lewisburg, and, with the assistance of the Rev. W. Shadrach, D.D., succeeded in securing a subscribed endowment of $100,000. Thus, while he had been signally successful in bringing the churches up to increased activity for the world's conversion, he was permitted, at the same time, still farther to promote that great end by laying the foundation of an institution from which, doubtless, many a young man will go forth to reap the precious harvests that are, even now, whitening every field of Christian effort.

CHAPTER XVI.

REOPENING OF BURMAH.

"Be wise now, therefore, O ye kings; be instructed, ye judges of the earth Serve the Lord with fear, and rejoice with trembling. Kiss the Son, lest he be angry, and ye perish from the way, when his wrath is kindled but a little."

Ps. ii: 10-12.

"Trust, trust the faithful God;
His promise is unfailing;
The prayer of faith can pierce the skies;
Its breath is all-prevailing.

Look! look! the fields are white;
And stay thy hand no longer;
Though Satan's mighty legions fight,
The arm of God is stronger."

The chief cause of Mr. Kincaid's prolonged visit in this country was the distracted state of the Burman empire. After the ascension of Thur-ri-wa-di to the throne—whose arbitrary policy was the immediate cause of Mr. Kincaid leaving Ava—the condition of the country, for a long time, was such as to render it impossible to occupy it as a field of labor, at least with any hope of extensive usefulness.

But, beside the contracted views of the government, so unsettled was the whole state of their political affairs, that it was impossible to calculate what would be the developments of the future, and the only course left, therefore, was patiently to wait the unfoldings of Providence.

Very soon, however, events began to transpire which awakened confident hope—that the day was near when that dark land would again be thrown open as a field for missionary effort.

The history of the revolution under Thur-ri-wa-di, his success, and the subsequent inglorious termination of his cruel reign, together with the encouraging prospect which it afforded of the reoccupancy of Burmah proper, was most graphically sketched by Mr. Kincaid immediately upon receiving intelligence of the overthrow of the revolutionists.

"The emperor of Burmah," he wrote, "is dethroned, and an entire revolution has taken place in the government. Prince *Mekara* is made regent, and the Woon-gee, who signed the Yandabo treaty, is associated with him in the new administration.

This change in the government will be hailed with rapture through all the provinces in the empire. No two men could be more unlike, than the *Mekara* prince and the deposed monarch—the one by nature a tyrant, and the other amiable and unambitious. I became acquainted with both these princes in 1833, and by both was treated with great kindness.

Thur-ra-wa-di manifested no interest in any conversation but such as related to the power, wealth, and political influence of nations. He pretended to admire France, Persia, and China, and never concealed his dislike of the English. No one could be with him long, without perceiving that his hatred of the English arose from his dread of their power. He took one of the daily papers printed in Calcutta, had it translated, and when he could fix upon any reverse or disaster, it seemed to afford him the highest gratification. He is five feet four inches in height, and well formed. His forehead is remarkably high and retreating, and his eyes brilliant and piercing. When pleased, his eyes are peculiarly fascinating; but when angry, they are lighted up with dreadful vengeance.

The *Mek-a-ra* prince is somewhat taller, but less muscular, and has a high, full forehead, with large, intelligent, and smiling eyes. When thoughtful and studious, there is a slight tinge of melancholy in his countenance, but in conversation there is a glow of kindliness spread over his whole face. His inquiries always turned upon religion, science, and literature. The philosophy of religion, or the great principles brought out and inculcated by different systems of religion, interested him deeply. Next, mathematics, astronomy, and languages, interested him. He is the most learned Burman in the world. To gratify his thirst for learning, he procured Rees' Cyclopedia and other works, a pair of large English globes, and a telescope, in which he can see the rings of Saturn, and the satelites of Jupiter. I gave him a copy of the Bible, and a copy of Gallaudet on the Soul, in the Burman language. Paul's epistle to the Romans interested him more than any other book. He often remarked on its profound reasoning, and on the great principles there brought out. Dr. Price had taught him to read English, but he was not able to speak it. At his request, Dr. Price commenced an English and Burman dictionary ; and after his death, it was taken up and finished by Mr. Lane, an English merchant, and printed at the expense of the Honorable East India Company.

The amiable and humane character of the *Mekara* prince is proverbial in Burmah.

Ko Gway, a venerable old man, who became a Christian, and afterwards deacon of the church in Ava, told me he was an eye-witness of a successful act of the *Mekara* in behalf of two state criminals. The men were leaders in a rebellion in one of the frontier provinces. They were brought to Ava and sentenced to be crucified. This sentence was carried into execution without the walls of Ava, a little after sundown. The next morning, very early, the prince, then about twelve years old, went out with his attendants and passed near where these two men were crucified. Hearing their agonizing cries, he inquired what it meant, and being informed, he directed his attendants to hasten with him to the palace. He threw himself at his father's feet, and with bitter tears, implored him to have mercy on the men. The king gave orders, instantly, to have them taken down. It was a little after sunrise when they reached the place, and their groans had become feeble, as life was fast ebbing away. The wood was sawed off each side of the feet and hands, and then the wood split, in order to draw out the great iron spikes ; the young prince all the time standing by, weeping and hurrying the men. The older of the prisoners was too far gone to be restored, and soon expired. The younger, being about thirty, revived, after all that horrible suffering, and in a few weeks was entirely cured. This act of humanity procured for him the respect and veneration of the whole empire.

Thur-ra-wa-di was proud, haughty, ambitious and cruel. It was well known in Ava, that persons whom he disliked had been betrayed within his compound, and murdered by his orders. Some of the most distinguished robber chieftains in the empire were known to be in constant communication with him, and had his protection ; but the fact that he was the king's own brother, and shared largely in the king's confidence, was a sufficient reason why no officer of government should venture to impeach him. It is true, this prince had some interesting traits of character, which, among a people like the Burmans, atoned for many faults. He was enterprising, enthusiastic, and generous in his temperament. Those whom he esteemed, he loaded with favors, and met with fascinating smiles. In February, 1837, a notorious robber chief, who had received for himself the title of *Kea-gee,* (the great tiger) was pursued by the government, and it was currently reported and believed, that he had taken shelter with the prince *Thur-ra-wa-di.* A messenger was sent from the *Lhoot dau* (the king's high court) to the palace of *Thur-ra-wa-di,* to inquire if *Kea-gee* was there. This was an insult which the prince could not brook. He took fire instantly, and used insulting and threatening language towards the court, at the head of which was the queen's brother, whom he hated, as he did the queen, with a deadly hate. The messenger fled back to the *Lhoot dau,* and without loss of time, an officer, with some eighty or a hundred men, was sent to search for the robber chieftain. The prince, aware of what was going on, armed between one and two hundrod of his men, and when the police arrived at his gate, and demanded admission, the prince ordered his men to fire. Two or three were killed, several wounded, and the rest fled precipitately to the *Lhoot dau.* This was open rebellion ; the whole city was in an uproar. *Thur-ra-wa-di,* taking his family and about three hundred men, forced one of the gates of the city, and seizing whatever boats they came to, crossed the river to *Sagaing*. Taking the governor of that city and a few hundred men, the prince went, by forced marches, to *Moke-so-bo*, a strongly fortified city, about fifty miles west of Ava.

He next sent messengers through all the provinces to report that the queen's brother had usurped the throne, imprisoned the king, murdered the heir-apparent, and was seeking to take his life ; and he called upon all to rally around his standard, and assist in putting down the queen's brother. The robber chieftains were despatched to collect their hordes of outlaws together. In a few days, he had about ten thousand armed men, and these were so placed as to cut off all communication between Ava and the provinces. He had his spies constantly circulating reports in Ava, magnifying the number of his forces, and repeating the solemn oaths he took before pagodas, that his only design was to put down the queen's brother, and restore the king to his rightful power. As the queen's brother was odious to the people generally, they were ready to believe any such report. This paralyzed the government ; for though the king soon had some thirty thousand troops, and the walls of Ava bristling with cannon, it availed nothing. The people thought that in fighting *Thur-ra-wa-di*, they were *really* fighting their king. So there was constant defection in the king's army. Early in May,

Ava was beleagured. On every side was a large army intent on plundering the capital. The *Mekara* prince was sent to intercede for the city. *Thur-ra-wa-di* insisted on giving it over to be sacked by his armies. Col. Burney, the English Resident, was requested by the king to use his influence to save the city from the awful calamity threatened. Nothing can exceed the anxiety and gloom that reigned through the city. All business ceased. Old men sat in groups, here and there, conversing mournfully. Mothers sat in their doors with their children nestled around them, listening to the thousand tales of outrage and cruelty committed without the walls the night before. The gayety of the Imperial city was gone. The walls were covered with troops, but no confidence was placed in them. All dreaded the approach of night, fearing an attack before morning. The appearance of Halley's comet, at this time, greatly increased the consternation.

The king was urgent for Col. Burney to interpose his kind offices. *Thur-ra-wa-di* himself, was still at *Moke-so-bo*, and Col. Burney proceeded to that city. He persuaded the prince to come and take charge of his armies, and after many interviews, he consented to spare the city. The keys of Ava were delivered to him, the king's troops were disbanded, and the whole empire was prostrate at his feet. To Col. Burney, under God, must probably be attributed the deliverance of Ava from one of the most fearful calamities that can befall a great city.

In a few days, the prisons of Ava were crowded with noblemen and officers, who had been attached to the old government. In violation of oaths and promises, the king was placed in confinement; the queen and her only daughter, about fourteen years old, were trampled to death by elephants; the queen's brother, after suffering the most horrible tortures, was put to death. Public executions took place almost daily, and hordes of robbers overrun the land. *Thur-ra-wa-di* tore in pieces the *Yandabo* treaty, and told Col. Burney that though he respected him as a man and as a British officer, yet as a Resident at the court of Ava, he did not know him. About the same time, he sent a special messenger to me, to inform me that I must neither preach nor give my sacred books to the people. The next day I waited on the new king, to learn from his own lips his intentions on a subject so momentous as the closing of his empire against the diffusion of Christian knowledge. I was received, as formerly, in the kindest manner, and he introduced the subject himself, in the presence of his whole court, by saying, 'The fates have made me king, and, therefore, I am *Tha-tha-na-da-ya-ka,* (defender of the faith) and must sustain the religion of the empire.' Much more to the same import he said as a reason for the course he had marked out for his government. It would reqnire too much space here, to give in detail the conversation, which filled up more than an hour. The next day I called, taking with me the Burman Bible, in four volumes. Some three years before, I had given the prince a copy of the New Testament. The king inquired, very pleasantly, 'What have you there?' 'The only book which the Eternal God has given to mankind,' I replied. He called an officer and directed him to take it to his private apartments. He went on to say, that he wished me to remain at Ava,—that I could teach science, and that he wished me to translate for him the History of England. I replied, that it was impossible for me to lay aside the office and work of a teacher of religion. The king's mind appeared to be made up that the Christian religion should not be taught, and my mind was equally made up to remain in Ava only as a teacher of Christianity.

To act covertly, and try to accomplish something secretly, was foreign to my feelings and in opposition to all my views of the spirit and genius of Christianity. We left Ava in sadness. We had seen a little church grow up within the walls of that ancient and proud city,—large numbers had become partially enlightened, and their minds favorably impressed with the principles of Christianity. Mrs. Kincaid was almost daily surrounded with females, who called to converse with her, and listen to her instruction. And the morning we left, a multitude of our old and familiar friends, as well as the church, thronged the shore, and when the parting words were uttered, not a few of them wept, bidding us not to forget them. The flood bore us on, and soon nothing was to be seen of the great city but the tall, glittering spires. The thoughts and feelings of that hour must remain unrecorded. *Ko Gway* and his wife, two aged disciples, who had endeared themselves to us by their amiable manners and tender solicitude for our happiness, spent a large part of the preceding day at our house, rendering whatever assistance they could. Several times they said, 'Teacher, we shall pray that God will change the mind of the king, or else take him away.' Such were the feelings and prayers of many. *Thur-ra-wa-di* had put to death the heir-apparent,—the queen,—her brother,—and a large number of the nobility and officers; all on whom there was the slightest taint of suspicion that they were favorable to the old government. He was not satisfied with removing the governors of provinces and cities,—the greater number of them were brought to Ava in irons and then beheaded. One with whom I had been a guest, the governor of *Mo Nheen*, a province near the borders of China, was brought to Ava in chains, and then fastened up to posts, and embowelled near a great thoroughfare just without the walls of the city; and when we left Ava, the 17th of June the bones were still hanging there, rattling in the wind. He was a venerable old man, and highly intelligent. In the preceding February, when on a tour through the northern provinces of the empire, I spent a night and a day in his house, and it was hard breaking away from him. His urbanity and kindness would do honor to a man in any country. On reaching my boat, I found his lady had sent a variety of articles for my journey. His only crime was attachment to the old king. Neither faithfulness nor fitness for office was regarded,—nearly all were swept away. Every thing indicated that *Thur-ra-wa-di* would secure to his family an undisputed throne. The Governor General of India took no notice of his spurning the English Resident from his court, and his trampling under foot the treaty of Yandabo ; but, after some months, sent up another officer of high distinction, Col. Benton, with a large amount in presents. The forbearance of the Governor General only increased his insolence. Col. Benton could not obtain an audience, and the bazaar people were punished for selling provisions to Col. Benton's servants, so that they were in danger of being starved. Col. Benton, with his suite, was obliged to leave. After this he raised an army of 100,000 men, and all well armed, proceeded to Rangoon, 500 miles from the capital. With such a vast army hovering near the provinces ceded to the English, and led on by the king himself, no small anxiety was felt. To watch the movements of this army, cost the Indian Government about half a million. After a few months' stay in Rangoon, the king, with his army, returned to Ava. A large part of his army was disbanded, but soon after he raised another of 100,000, and when about ready to march, the cholera broke out, spreading death and desolation through the empire.

Last summer the king appointed a successor to the throne. Passing by the prince of Prome, a young man of great energy and influence, but inheriting, in no small degree, the sanguinary temperament of his father, the king selected and installed as his heir, a son of feeble intellect. The prince of Prome was offended, and the Prime Minister, *Moung Dau Gyee,* manifesting too openly his partiality for the prince, was called to the palace. The king inquired if he was aware of the disaffection of the prince of Prome; the venerable old minister replied that he was. Instantly, the king rose and stabbed his minister to the heart. Losing all self-control, and apparently becoming insane, he killed a large number of his principal officers. The prince of Prome fled to the Shan provinces, east of Ava, but soon returned and was executed. Among the ministers murdered, is *Moung Gulla,* a young man of rare talents, and the most distinguished military man in Burmah. The remaining ministers and officers, fearing for their own safety, and regarding the king as insane, seized and confined him, and appointed a regency in which the *Mekara* prince has a conspicuous place, as also the old nobleman who signed the Yandabo treaty. Thus has fallen one of the proudest monarchs, and one of the greatest tyrants that ever sat on the throne of Ava. In eight short years he, with all his family, have passed from the summit of human ambition to a felon's home.

The probability is, that the pacific and enlightened principles of government pursued before the revolution in 1837, will be restored; that friendly relations will again be opened between Burmah and India; the odious and crushing monopolies removed, and commerce again flourish. The *Mekara* prince is not a statesman; but he is highly intelligent and enlightened, and withal, humane and generous. He has more knowledge of Christianity than any other prince in the empire, and is it too much to hope, that in mercy to the millions of Burmah, God has raised him to power? To me it seems to be a most merciful interposition of Divine Providence, and that the way is opening to publish in the great and beautiful valley of the Irrawaddy, the tidings of peace and salvation. Then over all the mountain districts of Burmah are thickly scattered the Karen villages, a people prepared, in a remarkable degree, for the reception of the gospel. Will the churches awake to more earnest prayer and vigorous effort? Will heralds of salvation say, '*send us?*' I wish to return, and I cherish the fond hope, that at no distant period, I shall be preaching the blessed gospel in the language of Burmah."

"Swiftly, on wings of love,
Jesus, who reigns above,
Bids us to fly;
They who his message bear
Should neither doubt nor fear;
He will their Friend appear;
He will be nigh.

When on the mighty deep,
He will their spirits keep,
Stayed on his word;
When in a foreign land,
No other friend at hand,
Jesus will by them stand—
Jesus, their Lord.

Ye who, forsaking all,
At your loved Master's call,
Comforts resign,
Soon will your work be done;
Soon will the prize be won;
Brighter than yonder sun
Ye soon shall shine."

CHAPTER XVII.

OFF AGAIN FOR BURMAH.

"He is a chosen vessel unto me to bear my name before the Gentiles, and kings."—Acts ix. 15.

"Yes! we would not here detain you,
But our daily prayers shall rise,
Earnest with the love we bear you,
While you toil where error lies.
Fervent pleadings,
For rich blessings from the skies.

Man of God, once more departing
Hence, to preach a Saviour slain,
With a full, warm heart, we give thee
To the glorious work again!
Faithful servant!
Thou with Christ shall rest and reign"

Though anxious again to engage in his loved work, serious doubts were entertained by many as to the practicability of encouraging Mr. Kincaid to reënter Burmah, or of making any direct effort, at that time, to regain the ground which apparently had been lost. For several years it had been confidently asserted and published, that Burmah was closed, and that missionaries would not be allowed to labor there.

Mr. Kincaid, however, believed that the time had fully come for resuscitating this mission, and, under a deep conviction of duty, he was led, in 1849, to ask from the Executive Committee, an appointment as a missionary to Ava. This request having been complied with, they were subsequently solicited to send a missionary-physician to the same field and at the same time. The brother who applied for the appointment, Dr. Dawson, besides the qualifications which might ordinarily be looked for in a candidate for such service, had the advantage of an intimate knowledge of the Burmese people and language. His appointment was urged on the ground that his medical skill would be likely to prove a shield to the mission, and was strongly pressed by nearly every pastor and many influential laymen in Philadelphia; the Committee, however, were unwilling to incur the expense and hazard of the experiment without special authorization from the Board. Accordingly, at the Annual Meeting of the Union, held at Buffalo in 1850, the whole subject was presented to the Board, and by them referred to a special committee who, through the Rev. Dr. Williams, made the following able report:—

"The subject," said they, "is one of grave import, and is not without its peculiar difficulties. The renewal of aggressive operations on the part of our missions against the heathenism of Burmah proper, has been for some years the theme of solicitude, discussion and prayer. It seemed a reproach on American Baptists, that whilst their labors had been drawn off or excluded from these territories, some members of the much older Romish missions remained in comparative security: although it was understood they so remained in virtual inertness, mute and bound, as to any efforts at proselytism. Our own labors among the Karens, a noble though a subjugated race of the population of Burmah, had been and yet are crowned with signal benediction. And the recent journals of Roman Catholic missions show, that to this field, in which our triumphs have far outstripped any Burman results of their labors, our success has provoked them, and in consequence, Romish priests are now going thither to rival, to thwart, and, if it may be, to supplant us.

A brother beloved, who, after long toil in the East, had been spending years amongst us, feeding and kindling missionary zeal in this his native country, finds himself now in a state to attempt the resumption of his eastern tasks; and his heart yearns to preach Christ at Ava itself, the imperial capital of Burmah. A large portion of his family will accompany him; and it is thought that their very presence, with the husband and father, will be to Burman suspicion a pledge of the honest and unworldly character of his mission. But, severed there, as this family would be from such medical relief as is accessible at many other mission stations, it seems desirable that they should not be sent out so unprovided in their perilous loneliness, and where sickness, so likely to befall them would, become doubly fearful and needlessly fatal. A brother who was in youth long a resident of that country, speaking several of its tongues, of approved medical skill, and a kinsman of the missionary, and himself of allowed piety and devotion, offers himself and family to attend the venture.—Brethren in Philadelphia, long the city of his residence, urge his appointment and most forcibly.

On the other hand, the Executive Committee at Boston find themselves surrounded by peculiar embarrassments. Recognizing the worth and medical skill and disinterestedness of the missionary physician, thus nominated for appointment, the brethren left in the keeping of our Mission Rooms are like Paul the Apostle, burdened with that charge, so anxious though so blessed a one: 'the care of all the churches cometh upon' them. They must look with earnest solicitude to the effect of every new station, established or reoccupied, upon the churches *at home*, as winning their decided sanction and support; and upon the missionary churches and laborers *abroad*, as it may propitiate their judgment, and as it may aid *their* work on the one hand, or on the other hand lessen and divide *their* resources.

Our churches in this country have spoken with some distinctness their opinion, that the press and the school and the tract may have sometimes crowded disproportionately on the old apostolic method—the simple preaching of Christ's word; and that the Executive Committee should therefore sedulously seek to restore the balance that may have been disturbed, between such ministerial and other forms of missionary labor. The physician in the present case would not go out as an ordained minister. Again, whilst opinions expressed on the part of some brethren, as our excellent brother Kincaid himself, and others more or less conversant with Burmah, favor the conclusion that Ava is open as a missionary station, several of our missionary brethren in Burmah itself seem to hold an opposite sentiment. If the doors of the imperial capital be found yet hopelessly sealed, the casting of the missionary enterprise which makes the experiment into so large and costly a shape, would be occasion hereafter of some regret if not complaint. It is allowed that, if the gates be found open, a physician may be himself one of the strongest commendations and safeguards at Ava to a preaching missionary. The Luke, "the beloved physician," may not only minister to the bodily infirmities of the Paul, but be the usher and defender and patron of the Apostle. But this is an uncertain result, remote and problematical; whilst the pecuniary burdens consequent upon the measure would be certain and immediate and permanent. The Executive Committee are willing that our brother Kincaid should go forward; and if on trial he find his hopes as to the accessibility of the capital to be warranted, that, upon his sending back the requisite statements, the appointment of the missionary physician should be made, and the entire missionary staff required at the capital be thus completed.

Now it is the duty of the churches of Christ to cultivate a holy spirit of enterprise, and a generous, trusting faith in the God whose promises were never small, and whose strength is not yet spent. But he is also a God of council, and would have his people walk wisely and in lowliness before him. Whilst he blesses the simple trust that is the best basis of missions, he does not approve the kindled imagination and the glowing and self-reliant impulses that are often mistaken for simple faith, but which may be more truly entitled the romance of missions. Ava must have great influence; and deserves from us great remembrance and greatest prayers. In the first preaching of his gospel, Christ bade the apostles begin at Jerusalem, the Ava of Judaism; and Paul, Christ's great apostle to the uncircumcision, yearned through weary years to visit Rome, the metropolis of that Gentilism which he especially sought to convert. To that Burman race for whom your missionaries have translated the Bible, and so long prayed and toiled—the imperial Ava is both a Jerusalem and a Rome,—the seat of civil dominion and the proudest fastness of spiritual delusion and despotism. But as God in the early ages of the church soon scattered the apostles *from* Jerusalem; and made some of the greatest triumphs over Gentilism to be won far away *from* Rome; so it may be in the labors of the nineteenth century upon heathen Burmah. The capital having early repelled, may long and obstinately exclude what the nation is yet to receive at other points more vulnerable, and through channels which no despotism can always guard and close. And while Faith is daring as against the world, she must be docile and submissive as before the Providence that wields the world and guides the church.

Your committee have felt the solemnity, the special difficulties, and the vast responsibilities that cluster around a wise decision of the pending question. Apprehending in the expected larger expenditures of the coming year requisite for existing appointments, a very heavy draught upon your treasury, they yet desire to extend, where God seems to beckon us to the work, the cords of the missionary enterprise. But if in stretching out these cords the churches do not actually lengthen them by enlarged zeal, contributions and prayer, then the cord so extended at one spot will be only tightened at another, and perhaps with the result at this latter point to cripple, and it may be to strangle, other branches of our missions where the station is less than the present, one of uncertain enterprise, and where the demands for help are loud, imperative and unquestionable.—Strongly as we may be attached to new enterprises of high adventure and large promise—and we are bound to them by every tie of Christian sympathy and pious hope—yet we must not forget that to the existing stations we are held not only by all those above-named ties, but by the added and stronger bonds of the explicit, solemn and repeated pledges we have given—pledges we can neither easily discharge nor innocently forget.

Some of your committee have leaned, therefore, to the recommendation of the Executive Committee, that our brother Kincaid's experiment be first made; and that the appointment of a physician be reserved as a contingency to depend on the success of the experiment at Ava. But to conciliate as far as possible the wishes of all, your committee have concluded to unite in recommending yet another modification. It is, that the Board now recommend to the Executive Committee, to appoint a missionary physician: but that, from a regard to the growing demand of the churches at home for preachers as laborers in the missionary field, this appointment of a physician be with the explicit condition, that if the attempt to plant a station at Ava should be in Divine Providence frustrated, then such physician's relations to this Board cease. In suggesting this, the committee would expressly protest against any misconception. They have formed from concurrent testimony a high estimate of the worth of the brother, of his medical skill, and of his pious consecration. But they understand that he would be at no loss to secure, in the British colonial or consular establishments, an appointment with higher remuneration than we can offer, and would not therefore incur pecuniary loss or wrong. On the other hand, our missions in the ceded provinces, apart from Burmah proper, do not, it is understood, require the increased burden of such medical laborer to be attached to the mission.

Your committee make, with great distrust and after protracted and anxious discussion, the preceding suggestions as affording what seemed the most feasible, harmonious and safe disposal of the question."

Following the reading of this Report, it was—

"*Resolved,* That the Board will sustain the Executive Committee, in vigorous efforts to resume missionary operations in Burmah proper, and will justify the Committee in the appointment of a medical helper, to accompany the Rev. Mr. Kincaid in his attempt to reënter that field, on such conditions as are suggested by the Report of the Committee of five on the part of this Board."

These instructions the Executive Committee, at once, complied with, and in the following July Dr. Dawson with his family, together with Mr. Kincaid and his family, embarked at Boston, on board the Washington Allston, arriving at Maulmain early in the year 1851. Writing from this point, under date of February 21, Mr. Kincaid reported, in substance, that with respect to the prospect of planting a mission in Burmah proper there seemed to be nothing which could be regarded as, on the whole, unfavorable. "There are difficulties," said he, "but they do not appear to be insurmountable." The reigning king who ascended the throne about three years previous to their arrival, manifested but little interest in the affairs of the government, and his Prime Minister was reported to be a "peculiarly bigoted Budhist." On the other hand, all persecution on account of religion had ceased, and the Christian Karens residing within the jurisdiction of Burmese authority were permitted to enjoy a comfortable degree of security and quietude. It was also rumored that there were, at that time, fifteen Burmese Christians at the capital, one of whom was an officer of the king, with a thousand men under his charge, and another connected with the king's household; which seemed to imply, if the king was acquainted with the facts, that he was not particularly hostile to Christianity.

Leaving Maulmain, the missionaries proceeded by the earliest conveyance to Rangoon, and writing from thence under date of March 10th, Mr. Kincaid says:

"After remaining eleven days in Maulmain, Dr. Dawson and I took passage in a schooner of thirty-one tons, manned by Mussulmans, and on the morning of the 5th reached Rangoon, now little more than one wide ruin. The fire last December destroyed about three-fourths of the old city. Not only so, but a great number of boats and several ships were burned. Many hundreds of families barely escaped from their houses with their lives. Building is rapidly going on, and hence all sorts of material and all kinds of workmen are in demand.

It being exceedingly doubtful about our being able to procure a house, we left our families in Br. Simons's house and came on to see what arrangements could be made. One street called *Ko-la-don*, that is, *Foreigners' Street*, was saved entirely from the fire. The buildings are owned and occupied by Armenians, Mussulmans, and Hindoos. We called at once at the house in which I had lived nineteen years ago, owned by a Hindoo. The old man is dead, but his son received me with great cordiality, and gave us a room to occupy while in the city. When we first landed, we showed ourselves at the custom house and got our baggage passed. A few hours after, we were sent for and questioned relative to our business; where we came from; the name of the ship; the name of the captain; what places we stopped at, if any; how many days we were in reaching Africa; how many days we remained there; how long in reaching Maulmain; how many days we remained there; how many languages we understood; and many other questions of a similar character;—and all was written down with great minuteness. The next day we were sent for again, and questioned relative to our object in coming into Burmah, and if we were 'Jesus Christ's men;' all of which was written down, and then read to us, and the inquiry put if it was written correctly. On Saturday we were sent for again, and questioned relative to Dr. Dawson's knowledge of medicine, and how many kinds of diseases he could cure. Upon this, Dr. D. brought a volume on Surgery, full of illustrative plates; this the officers examined with care, and another record was made.

On Sabbath morning the viceroy sent for me. I told the secretary to inform his Excellency that this was a sacred day and I could not attend to any worldly business. This, it seems, was satisfactory, but Lord's day evening, between 9 and 10 o'clock, the secretary came and said I would be called early in the morning, and was to be questioned in reference to my former residence in Ava. He manifested no small degree of anxiety, thinking they were contriving a plan to get me into difficulty. He is a fine young man, and appears to be a true friend, but he is very timid. Not long since, however, an English merchant was imprisoned and his feet put in the stocks, because his father had, as they alleged, written a letter against the government in one of the Calcutta papers. It cost him between five and six hundred rupees to get out of prison. Several foreigners have been imprisoned during the last six months on the most frivolous pretences, and money extorted from them.

Early this morning, I was called to the custom house and questioned in reference to the year I first came to Burmah, how long I lived in Rangoon, and how long in Ava, and other points of a similar character; and my answers were all written down. One could almost fancy himself before a set of inquisitors. One of the officers afterwards came and apologized; he said it was the order of the viceroy, or governor, and his authority was supreme. I replied that we had no objection to answer any questions the government was disposed to ask. All the officers whom I had formerly known, treated us with civility. The viceroy is a new man, as are also all the high officers of the empire. The temper and policy of the government have changed amazingly since the revolution in 1837. When I have had more experience I will write more definitely.

Ko Thah A, the venerable old pastor, has called on us two or three times; also two other members of the church. The news of our arrival spread rapidly over the city and into the neighboring villages, and many with whom I had formerly been acquainted called,—among them two young men who had been educated in Mrs. Kincaid's school at Ava. Armenians, Mohammedans, and Hindoos have visited us. A Jew from Bagdad has spent two evenings with us, listening to our account of the Messiah. * * *

I have as yet obtained no information about the church in Ava. There cannot be many members there; some have died, and I find eight of the Ava disciples now members of the churches in Amherst and Maulmain; one is in Arracan."

CHAPTER XVIII.

RESUMING LABORS.

"What man is he that feareth the Lord? him shall he teach in the way that he shall choose."—Ps. xxv. 12.

"Then on!—his joys cannot be dim,
Who, trusting, goes to seek the lost:
O there are coronals for him,
Who toils for Christ, nor shuns the cost."

THE special object of Mr. Kincaid's visit to Rangoon was to ascertain whether it was possible to secure a house there for the accommodation of his family. And having succeeded in his design, he returned at once to Maulmain. Soon after this, reports reached him and were extensively circulated through the city, that the Governor of Rangoon had proceeded with great severity against several persons who had shown him special favor during his brief stay there. These reports were generally regarded as true, and soon they were confirmed by letters from two English gentlemen. The young Hindoo who had given him a room in his house, had been thrown into prison and compelled to pay a fine of two hundred rupees. A writer had also been fined one hundred rupees; while an interpreter, Moung Poh Gyau, had his life threatened for daring to speak in his favor after he had left.

Under these circumstances, various opinions were entertained about the propriety of going to Rangoon in the face of such hostile measures.

To Mr. Kincaid's mind, however, this opposition did not appear sufficiently serious to interfere, in the least, with his plans; and, accordingly, he hastened his preparations to leave, and having engaged a schooner, they sailed on the 12th of April, and on the morning of the 16th were at anchor before the great wharf. The consternation consequent upon the arrival of the missionaries at Rangoon, and the difficulties that there immediately beset them, are thus related by Mr. Kincaid in his journal:—

"It was thought extremely doubtful," says he, "about our being allowed to land. On learning this I was anxious to get all on shore before there could be time to issue an order prohibiting our landing. I hastened back to the vessel, and in a short time both families were in the house of Captain Potter. We returned as soon as possible, sent our beds, chairs, and a few boxes of clothes to the custom house, but it was near evening before they were passed. Coolies were sent off with them to the house of Joe Alley, which we had rented before leaving Rangoon. When the old man saw the coolies loaded with baggage rushing into his compound, he and several servants raised a cry of alarm and forbade a single article being put into the house. I came just in time to prevent the coolies and baggage being thrust into the street. I remonstrated, told him that he could not break his promise, that it was now nearly dark, and that our ladies and children could not remain in the street. The poor old Mussulman stroked his long white beard and trembled like an aspen leaf. He was so agitated that he talked half Burmese and half Hindoostani, and kept saying, over and over, 'I am afraid,—I am afraid of the Governor,—Moung Kinge has been imprisoned and fined two hundred rupees, a writer has been fined one hundred rupees, and Moung Poh Gyau has had his life threatened and has gone mad,—and all on your account,—I am afraid, sahib." His looks, his actions, his voice, all told how dreadfully frightened the old man was. I told the coolies to put the things down and bring the remainder. The poor old man took hold of me in the most imploring manner, and begged me to have compassion on his grey beard. I told him I would stand between him and all harm. I was now here and the governor would harm no one on my account. At length he gave a sort of consent to let us sleep one night in his house. Long after dark we had all assembled in the house and spread our mats on the floor.

Early on the morning of the 17th I went with Dr. Dawson on board the schooner, and began sending our boxes of books, medicine and furniture on shore, fearing, from all we heard, that an order might come prohibiting the landing of the baggage. We were delayed about boats and coolies, so that our baggage did not reach the custom house till five o'clock, and but little of it was passed. Joe Alley was more frightened than ever; he sent his son in the evening with two bottles of rose-water, and told the governor that we had come into his house and he wished to get rid of us. The governor replied that he must send us off.

Early on Friday morning, the 18th, the governor came to the custom house with a large retinue, and we were summoned before him. There was a dense crowd, for his stern, oppressive course against every one who had rendered us any little service, had awakened the greatest interest to know how he would proceed now that we had come back with our families and baggage. Besides Burmans there was a large number of foreigners,—Mohammedans, Armenians, and the few English in the place. Without ceremony the governor began, in a loud, harsh tone, to question me about coming to Burmah. 'What have you come here for? Who invited you? Your object is to overturn the king's religion. You have been driven out of Burmah before. Who gave you permission to come here?' He went on in this style for several minutes.

As soon as he gave me a chance to speak I replied: 'Your excellency must be aware that when I lived in Ava I was on the most intimate terms with nearly all the officers of the government, and was treated with the utmost kindness by the Mekara prince and prince Thur-ra-wa-di. When I left Ava the king urged me to remain, or if I left, to return as soon as I could and bring a printing press and a physician. I promised to do so, and have now returned as the king directed. So far from being driven out of Burmah, the king urged me not to go away.'

His manner was at once changed. He began to expatiate on the beauties of Budhism, and said that my object was to overthrow it. After a good deal of this sort of thing, he said, 'You can remain here, but you must keep in the house and do nothing till I get word from Ava.' He then called a man who speaks Hindoostani as well as Burmese and understands a little English, and said, 'You must not enter a single house, or go abroad any where, without having this man with you.' I was told by several persons, not an hour after, that this man was one of the worst spies about the court, detested by all foreigners. Things looked dark, much worse than I had anticipated. As I had been requested to attend a funeral and conduct the services, I went away to put myself in readiness.

After we left, the governor expressed himself rudely and violently against me. He was much pleased to have Dr. Dawson remain, but before the whole crowd of people, foreigners and all, he said he would not mind putting me in irons. This threat ran like fire over the city. In a short time it reached me, and I do not know when I have felt such a rush of indignation. If he had said it to my face it would have been manly, but it was coward-like to stab me in my back. My first impulse was to go and tell him to his face how much contempt I felt for cowards and unprincipled tyrants. Then the funeral, with all its solemn lessons was before me, and the thought of the resurrection of the just and the unjust calmed my spirit. My second thought was to pass his cowardly threat in silence.

Poor old Joe Alley heard the news and was thrown into a paroxysm of fear. His beard seemed to become whiter, and he looked as pale as death. All he could say was, 'Go! go! go!' so piteously that I could not withstand him. So, promising to get a place for our baggage, and to bring no more to his house, I started off at once. Of course I paid no attention to the governor's order to take his interpreter with me. It was, in fact, making me a prisoner, and I would recognize no such relation.

From an early hour a highly respectable Mohammedan had been aiding us in every way he could. The governor noticed this in the afternoon and ordered him to be beaten. Instantly some three or four fellows pounced upon him, beat him in a savage manner, and kicked him out of the compound,—two hundred people looking on.

I went to five or six places to procure store room, as our baggage was being rapidly overhauled and tumbled unceremoniously out of the custom house. On Saturday it was all passed and stowed in Captain Potter's godown. During the day a number of respectable persons, Burmans and foreigners, urged us to go to the governor and 'speak sweet words to him,' but I resolved to seek no interview. On Monday, however, at the urgent request of many, we concluded to go, and started off, but learned on the way that the governor was in a terrible passion, and had that morning beaten a Mussulman terribly. At 5 o'clock, P. M., we set off again, but being informed that about an hour before the same man was beaten again so dreadfully that he was carried off to die, as all supposed, we postponed our visit. The next morning we started off again, and again turned back, having learned that the governor, that very morning, had had a serious quarrel with his principal wife. A report was current in the city on Monday evening and through the following day, that the governor had publicly threatened my life. I did not then, and do not now, believe there was sufficient ground for such a report. But, true or not true, I was fully satisfied that he was too cowardly to commit such an outrage, and would have cared little about it had it not reached my family.

We now relinquished altogether the idea of going to him, but about 7 in the evening word came from the governor requesting us to call. We resolved at once to go, though it was very dark and nearly two miles off. We found him in an inner apartment with two or three officers and a few servants. He treated us courteously and showed us several swords made by a Burman. He wished us to praise them, and really the workmanship was praiseworthy. He made many inquiries about my former acquaintance in Ava. After a little time we got into an animated conversation about men and things in the Golden City. I told him it was my intention to go up to Ava after the rains, to which he made no reply. We remained about an hour. When we were about leaving he said, 'I shall write to the king and make strong representations in your favor; but there is one thing you must promise, that is, to give no tracts to the people.' I did not ask him for permission to remain, I did not ask him to write to the king; still, I thanked him for his offer to write.

We had that very day rented the house formerly

occupied by Col. Burney, now owned by Moung Sa, an aged *Woon-gee* in Ava. Without our knowledge the agent came in to obtain the governor's sanction, which was given promptly. Then turning to us he said, 'That is a very suitable house for you.' All passed off very well. After spending a week of extreme anxiety the storm seemed to have spent itself.

* * * * * *

On the 3d of May a *Sera-dau-gyee* came, by order of the governor, to inform us that a royal message had that day arrived, that the king had heard with pleasure of the American teachers who formerly lived in Ava; he expressed a wish that they would be disposed to remain in Burmah, and that they might enjoy every possible favor. The Royal Secretary was attended by a large retinue, and he seemed much gratified that he was the bearer of such news.

The large hall in our house having been put in order, I preached in English and in Burmese the first Lord's day in May, and had about thirty hearers. The second Lord's day had about forty hearers; among them were three Karens residing about two days' journey from Rangoon. One of them has been two years in Br. Binney's school, and is an intelligent young man. He is the pastor of a church in the village where he lives. He inquired earnestly and affectionately after Br. Binney and Br. Vinton. In the evening we had a prayer meeting,—four prayers in

Burmese, one in Karen and one in English, also singing in the three languages. * * * *

Poor Moung Kinge died three days ago, and on the following day was followed to the grave by a large number of people. He was much respected by the entire community. This is the second man murdered by the governor since we came to Rangoon. One was whipped to death, and Moung Kinge was frightened to death. Since the day he was imprisoned, his life menaced, and the threat ferociously made that his wife and children should be made slaves and sent in chains to Ava, Moung Kinge has been sinking to an untimely grave. He had no fortitude, and the shock was too great. The bitter tears of his widow and children awaken in me emotions of unutterable detestation toward the brutal tyrant who has been the cause of so much suffering. Moung Kinge was guilty of giving Dr. Dawson and myself the use of a room seven or eight days; for this he has been frightened to death. Moung Poh Gyau has only just survived the savage treatment he received. Gladly would I have been in the place of those young men, and suffered all the indignities and cruel threats of the governor.

Ko A, the venerable old pastor, calls occasionally. He is in good health, but feeble with age. The members of the church are scattered in different villages, except a few superannuated members. Ko A is too feeble to labor. As yet I can write nothing very definitely with reference to the Karens in this and the neighboring province of Bassein. The greater number of the Karen churches are from forty to one hundred miles distant.

Thus I have given you a brief outline of events since we landed in this city one month ago. You will perceive that a great change has taken place toward us on the part of the government, much to the astonishment of all, Burmans and foreigners. We may meet with opposition, we may expect it, but still, with the Divine blessing, nothing is too great to be overcome. I preach just as openly as I ever did in any land. So far, we feel encouraged to hope that the Lord has heard our prayers, and the prayers of his people, in behalf of these millions. Pray for us that we may be wise in winning souls to Christ."

CHAPTER XIX.

HAVING FAVOR WITH ALL THE PEOPLE.

"When a man's ways please the Lord, he maketh even his enemies to be at peace with him."—Prov. xvi. 7.

* * * "Seeking this
Alone—the approbation of his God,
Which still with conscience witnessed to his peace."

IN addition to the order from Ava which reached Rangoon on the third of May, and to which reference has been made in the preceding chapter, the governor subsequently received another communication from the king, and Mr. Kincaid was immediately summoned by the viceroy to listen to the reading of the royal letter. When he presented himself before him there was a full court assembled, and all business was at once suspended, while a secretary, by the governor's direction, read the paper aloud. The substance of the document was that, "the American teachers should be allowed, if they wished, and at any time that they might choose, to come up to the *golden feet;* or, if they preferred remaining in Rangoon, they were not to be molested."

After the reading of this royal order, the missionaries at once commanded universal respect. "You can hardly fancy," says Mr. Kincaid, "the altered tone of the officers and people towards us. Before these orders came down they were proud, haughty, and insolent. Even the coolies in the street would take pains to jostle us, and the underlings in office were insolent in the extreme. Nothing of this now. This order from Ava was unsolicited and unexpected. We cannot regard it in any other light than as a special indication of Divine providence to go forward in our work.

Our object in coming to this country," writes Mr. Kincaid, "is well understood. The governor himself said, last April, that he had formerly known me in Ava, and that I was laboring to overturn the king's religion. On the first of July, when we went to the governor's, we found some twenty-five or thirty officers and servants sitting in the audience hall. They began conversing among themselves on the subject of our mission, the character of our books, and the peculiarities of our religion; and, certainly, they said much that was very true. After this they began to ask questions, and one was, if we were not 'Jesus Christ's men.' 'We are,' I said, 'and now I will give you the reason;' and I went on for some twenty-five minutes giving them an outline of the Christian religion, no one interposing.

On the 29th of July we received a message from the governor, which gave us no little solicitude. Very early in the morning, one of the government interpreters came and said the governor expected to see us. What,' I inquired, 'does the governor want?' 'He says, sir, that he has been very kind to you, in sending up a petition to the king, and at great expense in bringing the royal order from Ava, and you do not visit him nor say anything about the expense of getting down the order.' 'Indeed,' I said, 'this is strange. If the governor sent a petition to the king he did it without our request; and who supposes it has cost anything to bring the order from Ava? It is an outrage to speak of expense, and you may tell the governor so.' 'No, sir, I would not dare to speak such words, for he is the governor, and you had better come and see him.' 'Very well; we will see him, but not to-day.'

Every one supposed that a demand would be made for some two or three hundred rupees—this would be treating us as he treats other foreigners. 'What will you do?' was the inquiry of every one. 'Refuse to pay any such demand.' 'But he has power to compel you.' 'He has power to send us out of the country, but he has not power enough to compel us to submit tamely to extortion and oppression.' We remained quietly at our work till the 31st, thinking it not best to be in haste to see him. Many persons who are very friendly, urged that we should go with a present worth thirty or forty rupees, tell him that we were afraid and that we were poor, and so throw ourselves upon his clemency. To this I replied that neither was true. We were not afraid, neither were we so poor as to beg. If the governor had any just claim we would pay him, but would never tamely submit to extortion and tyranny. For in submitting to one act of tyranny we were only inviting outrage and oppression.

We took along with us a small present worth about eight rupees. We were received in a bland and gentlemanly manner. The governor made several inquiries, and among others when we intended going to Ava; to which I replied, 'As soon as the rainy season is over.' 'You are right,' he said, 'it is dificult and dangerous to go up during the rains. When you are ready to go, I shall furnish you with the expense of the journey.' None who saw and heard him on this occasion, could fancy him the governor we had to deal with last April."

While disposed to be somewhat conciliatory in his personal relations, he seemed anxious also to convey an impression that his views were, to a degree changed respecting Christianity; and speaking to Mr. Kincaid one day on this subject, in the presence of the court, he said :—

"One thing about your religion I do not like; it aims

like ; it aims to destroy every other, and this is uncharitable. *They* allowed our religion to be good, but *we* would not allow theirs to be good ;" this was his great objection. To this Mr. Kincaid replied,

"That the whole design of Christianity was to bring the race of man to love God supremely, and to love others as themselves, and that this doctrine does certainly make men wise and good and happy."

"You are getting all the people over to your side, said the governor, "for you make them think well of yourselves, and of your doctrine."

One of the highest in rank among his officers said, "These teachers have all sorts of books ; and then they have maps of all the countries in the world, and globes that represent the earth as round as an orange, and that it turns round every day, and that the sun stands still. Does not this go to destroy Gaudama's religion ?"

"True," said the governor ; "this makes our religion false."

"Whether the sun goes round the earth," Mr. Kincaid replied, "or the earth round the sun, is a question that belongs to science and not to religion."

Everything, now, seemed to favor Mr. Kincaid in his work, and, full of faith, we find him engaging, at once, in active efforts not simply for the evangelization of Rangoon, but for the spread of the gospel through the whole length and breadth of the empire.

The scattered members of the Burman church now began to gather round him—numerous cases of inquiry began to appear—representatives of churches from distant towns came in to express their congratulations, others called to solicit books, and on every hand, he was permitted to see the most cheering tokens of the Divine favor.

Having sent off two of the native brethren to visit the Karen churches east of Rangoon, and also to the north and northwest, they zealously fulfilled their missions, and returning brought the most cheering intelligence of what they had been permitted to hear and witness of the grace of God.

Among other matters of interest, they reported that in every Christian household they found them maintaining family worship morning and evening, and on each Lord's day they met four times for public service.

The news of Mr. Kincaid's arrival in Rangoon, they found had preceded them, and hearing of his rough treatment by the authorities, prayer was made incessantly for him that he might not be driven from the country. In one village they spent a Lord's day with a church numbering over four hundred members, and when they met with these brethren and read to them the letters containing assurances of being affectionately and constantly remembered in the prayers of the teachers, all were affected to tears, and many wept aloud for joy. From the pastor of this church they bore to Mr. Kincaid the following simple and touching letter :—

" May the grace and fellowship of the Father, Son and Holy Spirit be with you, with my love, and the love of all the sons and daughters of God in this church. I am one of the least of all the disciples, and know but little of the divine word. Divine grace has made me a teacher of the gospel, and by the sacred imposition of hands I am made a pastor. Daily I study the Bible, and pray for a larger measure of the Holy Spirit, so as to teach and guide this flock of little ones. I have but little knowledge and can teach only what I know. I, the pastor, and all the church rejoiced greatly when we heard that you had come into this Burman kingdom, and cease not to pray for you. Our Father who is in heaven will hear our prayers. We all desire greatly to see you, and to hear more fully the deep things of God, that we may grow and be established in every virtue."

The ardent love of the Karens for the gospel was never more strikingly illustrated than in the efforts and sacrifices which many made, about this time, to possess portions of the word of God. Some came from a great distance, through districts infested with robbers and amidst almost incessant storms. Among these, Mr. Kincaid makes special mention of two Christian boys from the province of Pautanau, one hundred and thirty miles distant. They had been sent by the church with a letter requesting ten New Testaments, a copy of Pilgrim's Progress, seven tracts, and two hymn-books. The books were carefully rolled up and put in the bottom of a basket, and then the basket filled with rice and dried fish. This done, they gave the parting hand, and in a tremulous voice said—"Pray for us that we may be delivered from the calamity of falling into the hands of officers with these books."

Toward the close of this year, cases of inquiry began to multiply, and a number of hopeful converts soon presented themselves for the ordinance of baptism. One of these, in relating the exercises of his mind, said that about three months previous, his heart had been very much perplexed through a dream; he imagined himself going toward Shway Dagong, and when not far off, it crumbled down into a mass of ruins. He woke up in great distress, feeling that all his life long he had been rendering the homage, due only to God, to that senseless mass of ruins. He betook himself to prayer and the reading of the New Testament. The light of truth shined in upon his soul and he found peace in believing.

"Our baptism," says Mr. Kincaid, "took place between three and four in the afternoon, in the royal tank. a beautiful, clear sheet of water, nearly four miles in circumference. It has several finely wooded islands, and is surrounded on three sides by groves having a park-like appearance. Under the deep, dark foliage of a clump of aged trees, on a green bank sloping down to the water's edge, with the glittering spires of a hundred pagodas before us, we kneeled in prayer to Him who said, 'Lo, I am with you.' I cannot express to you our feelings when these redeemed ones, four Burmans and five Karens, went down into the baptismal grave, rendering homage to Him who is 'the resurrection and the life.'

We have a number of very earnest inquirers. Three of them, we think, have received the word of God into their hearts. There are, besides, a large number who no longer attempt any defence, but listen and are thoughtful. Just now, while I write, three men from Dalla are sitting by me in conversation on the character of Christ's religion. I have been reading and explaining to them for an hour. They are saying, 'Gaudama cannot stand, and what is the use? We are a poor, ignorant people, after having Gaudama's religion a thousand years.' An intelligent young priest, who has visited us repeatedly during the last three months, and has borrowed books of us, said the other day, that he was disgusted with the yellow robe and must throw it away. The fields are white for the harvest on every side of us. There is no serious opposition. People of all ranks and ages come to us. A few days since, an officer of high rank, with his lady and some twenty-five or thirty attendants, spent the evening with us, and gave us a very urgent invitation to visit them."

'Tis now the time of strife and war,
  The contest sounds on every side;
Nations are bound to Satan's car,
  And who shall meet him in his pride?

Is there no arm his power to break?
  Are there no hearts that deeply feel?
Sons of the kingdom! rise, awake!
  Obey at length your Saviour's will.

* * * * *

Hark! 'tis the trumpet's warning cry!
  Lo, o'er the earth the banners wave;
The Lord of glory comes from high,
  To rule, to conquer and to save.

CHAPTER XX.

LABORS INTERRUPTED BY WAR.

"In the time of trouble he shall hide me in his pavilion: in the secret of his tabernacle shall he hide me; he shall set me up upon a rock. And now shall mine head be lifted up above mine enemies round about me: therefore will I offer in his tabernacle sacrifices of joy; I will sing, yea, I will sing praises unto the Lord."—Ps. xxvii. 5, 6.

"Labor! Wait! though midnight shadows
Gather round thee here,
And a storm above thee lowering
Fill thy heart with fear—
Wait in hope! the morning dawneth
When the night is gone,
And a peaceful rest awaits thee,
When thy work is done."

DURING a residence of more than six months in Rangoon, Mr. Kincaid was cheered by scenes and incidents of extraordinary interest; but in the midst of these encouragements, and when he had nearly completed his preparations for proceeding to the capital in pursuance of his original purpose and under favor of the royal invitation, a new aspect was put on the posture of things by the arrival of war steamers at Rangoon, demanding on behalf of the East India Government redress of grievances. For a long time, British subjects had suffered from the Burman Government the greatest injustice. Without cause, they had often been fined and imprisoned, and, such was the terror under which they were living, that they were compelled to endure these wrongs in silence, knowing that the slightest whisper of dissatisfaction would only be visited by ten-fold greater outrages, and even with cruel tortures and death. At length tidings of the doings of the government towards British subjects reached the ear of Commodore Lambert, and, after taking the necessary steps to satisfy himself of the truth of these reports, he came to demand redress of the Burmese authorities.

On the evening of the 24th of November, 1851, a frigate and four armed steamers came before the city and immediately every thing was thrown into the utmost state of alarm. The governor threatened to set the city on fire, and in every house the foreigners were at work securing their papers and property. Great gongs were beating in every direction. A report was current that all who wore hats (Europeans) would be seized and carried off as hostages. Near midnight Mr. Kincaid was sent to go to the governor's, nearly two miles distant. Without hesitation he set off, but was met by messengers countermanding the order

On the following morning the governor with a large guard appeared on the wharf, and there issued an order that any person, foreigner or native, who should come down to any of the wharves, or appear on the bank of the river, should be instantly beheaded. This order was published through the city by beat of gong and public crier. On hearing this Mr. Kincaid went immediately to the main wharf, where there were several distinguished officers and a guard, and remonstrated with them in strong terms on the insane course they were pursuing,—working themselves and the people into a panic, when there was all possible evidence that the ships were come on a peaceful mission,—to prevent, not to make war. They felt it, but were disposed to be blind to the innumerable acts of injustice and cruelty inflicted on all classes of people.

Com. Lambert having sent a deputation of four officers with a communication to the viceroy, he immediately called for Mr. Kincaid; and in the presence of some fifty of his great chiefs, he desired to know from him whether the translation of the commodore's letter was correct. After carefully reading both he was assured that it had been faithfully rendered.

"What does it mean?" said the governor. "I am accused of being a bad man, committing outrages on her Britannic Majesty's subjects, and yet the letter does not specify in what way I have done this. Tell me what I should do."

"I am not competent," said Mr. Kincaid, "to advise in these matters."

"Do not tell me so," he said; "you have more books and maps than all the other people in the city, and you know what the English want and what I can do."

To get rid of his importunity Mr. Kincaid said,—"You can write to the commodore and ask for an explanation." This struck him favorably. Then he inquired whether the English had come for peace or war.

"For peace, undoubtedly," Mr. Kincaid replied. "If they had come for war, instead of three ships they would have had twenty-five or thirty."

"After a few days," says Mr. Kincaid in his journal, "the governor recovered in some measure from the panic into which he was thrown, and commenced hostile preparations, buying up all the muskets in the city, collecting guns from all the neighboring cities and fortifying the heights of *Shway Dagong*, and building stockades at *Kee-men-ding*, four miles above the city. He has collected from the surrounding villages about ten thousand men, and has invited to his aid a celebrated robber chief with all his followers, thus getting together all the desperate characters in the lower provinces. As yet we had felt safe in the old city, as the majority of the inhabitants are foreigners, but on the 4th and 5th of December orders were issued, it was reported, to attack the foreigners, plunder them, cut their throats, and burn the city. Bodies of armed men and of desperate character were constantly parading the streets. Foreigners were all armed and keeping ceaseless watch in their houses. Com. Lambert very kindly gave me an invitation to place the ladies and children on board of one of his vessels, and the stern cabins of the steamer 'Tenasserim' were prepared for them; but Capt. Barker, of the 'Duchess of Argyle,' a large merchant ship, invited us to take refuge on his vessel, which seemed preferable, as the ships of war were threatened with an attack by fire-rafts. On the evening of the 5th we took Mrs. Kincaid and Mrs. Dawson, with the little children, to a private wharf, where a boat was ready to take them on board the 'Duchess.' The next day the young ladies went on board. Dr. Dawson and myself remained on shore most of the time. We packed up our books and the most valuable part of our baggage, and placed them in fire-proof godowns belonging to Mr. Birrell. The ladies and children were now safe and there was little danger to our property from fire, but it was necessary to keep a constant watch, especially by night, as the governor threatened to let loose the robbers, now about 500 strong. He had openly and repeatedly declared his intention of taking the lives of eight persons whom he named, among whom I was included. We regarded his threats as the ravings of a madman; still I kept away from the new city, for I knew if he should muster courage to commence hostilities he would be anxious to have me for a translator and interpreter.

* * * * * *

A little after dark on the 10th of December, as I was passing along one of the principal streets, I was suddenly seized by some eight or nine Burmans, who partly carried, partly dragged me into a dark, narrow lane. There I was surrounded by forty or fifty armed men. A long and not very pleasant altercation followed,—they threatening me, and I in turn threatening them; they insisting on taking me to the governor, and I insisting on going to the custom house. At length I got to the custom house—I hardly know how. A bundle of clothes from the washerman, which a Burman carried after me, was the excuse for this outrage. The custom house officers interfered, and after a long dispute these guards went to the governor for an order to take me out. It was nearly two miles to the governor's, and while they were gone the custom house officers hurried me off on board ship.

This, it seems, annoyed his excellency, for the next afternoon he sent an officer to the commodore, complaining that I had taken my family on board ship without his permission, and so had broken the laws of Burmah. Com. Lambert replied that that law might hold in reference to Burman subjects, but not in reference to British subjects or persons claiming British protection. He drew up a letter and sent it to the governor by one of his officers and Mr. Edwards, his translator, in which he stated, that the amity existing between the government of the United States and her Britannic Majesty rendered it imperative on his part to demand of his excellency the punishment of those men who had seized and maltreated me the evening before in the streets of Rangoon. The governor expressed much regret at what had taken place, and said the men should be punished if I would point them out. Of course this was impossible, for the men were withdrawn from the old city.

On the 12th I went on shore again. I have learned that two Portuguese, the tools of a Jesuit, have made the governor believe that I am at the bottom of the English expedition. This is the secret of his hostility to me. Within a few days the governor of Dalla has received orders from Ava to place his troops at the disposal of the Viceroy of Rangoon. Accordingly, fifteen hundred men crossed the river early on the morning of the 19th, uttering the most savage yells. Yesterday one thousand men arrived from Prome. After all, the only men the governor can depend on are the robbers. The peasantry, that make up four-fifths of his army, will throw away their muskets and run at the firing of the first gun. The officers threaten the Karen Christians that they will place them 'in the fore front of the battle' if the English come on shore. Three hundred of the disciples are now on duty at the great pagoda. The churches are sending messengers to us almost daily to inquire how things are and to let us know their situation. Few of them sleep in their houses for fear of robbers. Our hearts bleed for them. We can only say to them, Look up to Him who took care of Elijah in the desert. The Burman peasantry, heathen as well as Christian, are also sending messengers to us, expressing the hope that the English will put an end to the brutal tyranny under which they have so long suffered. Among our more than ten thousand disciples, besides hundreds who are 'almost Christians,' there is earnest prayer to Him who ruleth over all.

It is a merciful Providence that we had not left for Ava. We had procured one boat and were just settling the price of another, when the war ships arrived. The Lord hath ordered all things well."

All efforts to bring the Burmese authorities to terms having failed, hostilities ensued, and the mission families, in imminent peril, were compelled to hasten their escape from the city. "We had only one hour," says Mr. Kincaid, "to abandon our house and take refuge on ship-board. With hardly a change of clothes, we fled. One hour more, and we would have been prisoners. Many foreigners did not escape, and they were loaded with irons and crowded in a loathsome prison. Some died under their sufferings, and the others were repeatedly ordered out for execution and then remanded to prison."

As it was impossible to calculate how long these hostilities would continue, the missionaries deemed it prudent to seek a refuge in Maulmain. After remaining there about three months, however, Mr. Kincaid, leaving his family behind him, determined to return to Rangoon. The very day after his arrival the war was virtually terminated by the destruction of the great fortress which had been defended by 30,000 Burmans with over two hundred mounted guns. "From seven o'clock in the morning till evening of that day," says Mr. Kincaid, "I spent in the field-hospital among the wounded and the dying. At night I walked back two miles to the ship, among the dead and dying Burmans strewed over the battle-field. That was a terrible day, and I thought continually of our suffering disciples. After all, their sufferings had hardly begun. The great Burman army was shattered into fragments, and now, in groups of from one to three hundred, they were ravaging the country, burning the villages, slaughtering the cattle and robbing the people. I took up my abode in an old building, having a great number of idols in it. Having cleared out the idols and cobwebs, one large room was converted into a chapel. A Karen deputation found me the third day after the great battle; and then there was coming and going in one continued stream. The Burman disciples, also, came in from their various hiding places, and with them many other Burmans took refuge under my building."

In the following June, Mr. Kincaid was again joined by his family from Maulmain, and, having set things in order, every department of missionary work moved on as they never had seen it before. The people's hearts were softened like wax. The arm of the Lord was made bare, and they had Pentecostal seasons almost every week.

"In our missionary work," said Mr. Kincaid, "we have every encouragement to labor in season and out of season. We have baptized every Lord's day since the middle of July, and the whole number up to the present time is sixty. From several villages where we sent preachers and school teachers, we have cheering accounts. Two entire villages have sent off their poongyees, turned their buildings into chapels and school-houses, and sent to us a request to be taught the ways of God more perfectly. As soon as the war closes, there should be missionary stations at Danabo and Prome, two families for each.

Within a few days past we have buried two of our Christian women, one of them the oldest member of the church. As near as we can learn, she was ninety-three years of age. Till the very last she retained her mental powers remarkably. She possessed much faith, and spoke often of her desire to depart and be with Christ. At our last communion season she was borne to the chapel, and at the close expressed her joy at being once more permitted to unite in this holy service. Five members of the church have died within the year."

Writing about this time to Mr. Marshman, of Serampore, editor of the *Friend of India*, he said:—
"The principles of Christianity have taken deep root in the hearts of some 12,000, and through these a large amount of moral influence is brought to bear on some 20,000 more. Our churches are found scattered all the way from the seaboard to Prome. We have now at school in this city two hundred and fifty young persons preparing to go back to their villages, some to teach school and others to labor as evangelists among their countrymen. About forty native preachers are now supported by congregations over the country. The intelligence of recent events in Burmah has aroused to new energy the friends of missions in America, and I have no doubt but we shall be well sustained by having true and faithful men sent to our aid. I hope to see churches raised up along the whole line of this river to the *Hukang* valley. Then we shall stand on the borders of west-

ern China and on the upper waters of the great Cambodia, and can reach by our books and our preaching untold millions in the centre of eastern Asia. I almost wish that I had been born thirty years later in the Christian era, so as to see Christianity pouring its light over these vast regions.

CHAPTER XXI.

SETTING UP THE STANDARD AT PROME.

Go through the gates; prepare you the way for the people; cast up, cast up the highway; gather out the stones; lift up a standard for the people."
Isa. lxii. 10.

"Fear not, shrink not, though the burden
Heavy to thee prove;
God shall fill thy mouth with gladness,
And thy heart with love."

FOR many years the city of Prome, occupying a position midway between Rangoon and Ava, had been regarded as one of the most promising centres of missionary labor in the Burman empire. The gospel was first preached there by Dr. Judson, in 1830, and with an encouraging prospect of success, but after a residence of a few months, he was peremptorily ordered away. From that time to 1853 but little effort had been made to spread the knowledge of Christ among its 50,000 idolatrous inhabitants. In the beginning of that year, we find Mr. Kincaid taking up his abode there, and, in strong faith, laying his plans for its evangelization. By the kind assistance of the quarter master general of the army, he succeeded in obtaining possession of two monasteries, with a zayat immediately contiguous to the highway, and on Lord's day the 22d of January, he held his first public religious service. Much to his joy he soon ascertained that a Burmese Christian had anticipated him, and was already "holding forth the word of life," having nightly gatherings of the people at his house, to whom he read and explained the Scriptures. This man was one of the converts baptized ten years previously by Mr. Kincaid in Arracan, and was now in the employ of the assistant commissioner at Prome. He had entered into this service on the express condition that he might be allowed to spend a part of his time daily in giving religious instruction to his countrymen. From him Mr. Kincaid received a considerable amount of important information relative to the state of the public mind, and the best means of presenting before the people the claims of Christianity.

"Religious services," said Mr. Kincaid, "are held every Lord's day, at 11, A. M., in the chapel in the centre of the city. The congregation numbers from one hundred to one hundred and fifty, who are attentive listeners. Besides these, there are sometimes nearly a hundred comers and goers, who listen outside all around the chapel. After the regular services have closed, many of the hearers usually remain, and others also come in The disciples scatter themselves among them; and, collecting in little groups of five or ten, commence, in a conversational way, to lay before them the claims of Christianity; there they remain for an hour or two. This is often a time of great interest, and much excitement, as all are engaged in conversation. Sometimes a reference is made to the 'law and the testimony;' and the large quarto Bible is taken from the bamboo stand and placed on the floor, where it is read, passage after passage, by some one of the native assistants, and then explained in the hearing of all.

The assistants occasionally have meetings at their houses, in the north part of the city, and by this means the light of the gospel is spreading in their neighborhood."

The first fruits of the gospel at Prome were three converts, baptized February 22. In July, the number had increased to thirty-eight, and there were very many inquirers, not only in Prome, but in the neighboring towns and villages. In one village, ten miles distant, there were seven converts, and the entire village had abandoned their Budhist priests. Applications for preaching were received from other directions. Excursions had been made to large cities, sometimes by the missionaries, accompanied by the assistants, and sometimes by the assistants alone. At Keaugen, forty miles below Prome, with a population of sixty thousand, multitudes gave ear to the gospel.

In January there were four churches, including two Karen, and the near promise of a fifth, where five converts had been baptized, and there were several hopeful inquirers. The whole number received to baptism was about eighty, residing in ten or twelve localities, distant from Prome, in opposite directions, from twelve and thirty-eight, to ninety miles. Two of the baptized were from Ava, who came for the purpose of learning more of the way of life. Seventy members were enrolled on the records of the Prome church, of whom, twenty-one were Karens.

In a letter dated Prome, February 7, 1855, Mr. Kincaid says:

"We intend soon to make Tau-yet, forty-five miles north of Prome, one of our principal stations. It is four miles below Meàday, the frontier English fortress, and is rapidly becoming a large town. Innumerable villages cover the country in the rear of Keyau Gen. This we shall also make an important centre. We have encouragement to hope that three men, a short time since baptized, will become laborers in the Lord's vineyard. They are men of fair natural talents and a good education, and are studying the Scriptures day and night, so as to be able to teach others the things of the kingdom. One of the most encouraging features in the work of grace in Prome is the large proportion of gifted men and women, who are hopefully converted. There is one, and often there are two public meetings every evening in the city, conducted mostly by Ko Dway and Moung Pau-te. Very often the place is crowded, and not unfrequently some are obliged to go away for want of room. Moung Kauye, Moung Myat Poo, and Keyau Gen are almost constantly going from village to village, and from city to city, preaching Christ. If, within a few months, the Lord gives us three more evangelists, we shall be able to enlarge our field of active labor. In a few days I intend going north, and I hope to preach Christ in every city and village as far as Ava. Every week we have inquirers from northern cities, and we must heed the Macedonian cry.

Our hope and prayer is that the Lord will raise up laborers to reap this great harvest. I feel oppressed beyond utterance, when I look over this wide field and see what is to be done. It is important that we employ all the sanctified talent within our reach, for evangelizing these cities and villages."

Writing six months subsequent to this, he says—
"The word of grace is still onward. Several have been baptized within a few weeks, and among them one Chun, the first Christian of his race. Another Chun is a candidate for baptism. The Yoma mountains are inhabited by this people for hundreds of miles. They are evidently a branch of the great Karen family.

Our congregation on the Sabbath varies from one

hundred and fifty to two hundred. The church is preparing to build a good teak chapel during the coming dry season. They are subscribing liberally for the purpose.

Our Karen field is large to the northeast and southeast; and the spirit of inquiry is increasing. We have baptized over forty Karens, and are instructing eight for teaching schools in the villages, and two for assistants more particularly. Karen chiefs are often coming in and asking for school-teachers: but we have only one man who can read his own language. We hope to have ten more soon. There is a wide spirit of inquiry among this people, and the coming cold season I intend visiting two or three scores of their villages. We have disciples now in four cities between this and Ava."

But this religious prosperity was not confined to Prome. In every direction the influence of the gospel was spreading, and converts were multiplied in all the adjacent towns and villages. That which gave special and preëminent interest, however, to the work of grace at Prome, was that it included an unusual number of *Burmans*. Thus while the aggregate of baptisms at the close of the year was one hundred and sixty-one, more than one hundred were reported as Burmans.

"Full many a day in faith and prayer
Where heathen feet have trod,

Thou'st labored with a father's care
  To point their souls to God.

And O what joy thy spirit felt,
  When at the Saviour's feet,
With thee the anxious heathen knelt,
  God's mercy to entreat;

Or when beneath the yielding wave
  Of Irrawaddy's tide,
Burmah's dark sons allegiance gave
  To HIM, the crucified.

Go on, dear servant of the Lord,
  And still his love proclaim,
Till Burmans all may read his Word,
  And praise his holy name."

CHAPTER XXII.

IN FAVOR WITH THE KING.

"Seest thou a man diligent in his business? he shall stand before kings."
Prov. xxii. 59.

"Let us then, be up and doing,
With a heart for any fate;
Still achieving, still pursuing,
Learn to labor and to wait."

THOUGH Ava was the field to which Mr. Kincaid had been specially designated, various circumstances conspired to delay his going thither, and, while waiting for a favorable opening, he had been led, as we have seen, to devote himself to missionary labors in Rangoon and Prome. During the month of September, 1855, however, he was called upon by a messenger from the king and heir-apparent to ascertain when he intended to make his visit to the Royal City. Subsequently he received repeated messages from the court, which had now been removed to Ummerapoora, offering boats and men to take him and his family up, and also to furnish him with a house. Encouraged by this indication of good feeling on the part of his majesty, Mr. Kincaid, in company with Dr. Dawson, decided to make an experi mental visit to the Capital in the early part of the ensuing year,—this time being selected in view of the fact that they would then meet the Chinese and Shan caravans, and thereby have an opportunity of sending books widely over the northern and eastern provinces.

The journey to the Capital was begun on the 24th of March and accomplished on the 11th of April, some time having been spent on the way in visiting the most important villages and towns. Ummerapoora is situated a short distance above Ava, containing a population of 300,000 souls, and may be regarded, perhaps, as one of the finest cities in the Empire. The streets are broad and clean, and some of them are five or six miles long. On the north side of the city is a beautiful lake, and the cocoanut tamarind, mango and other trees, are to be seen in abundance.

One of the first things Mr. Kincaid did after getting his things out of the boat, was to dispatch the two native assistants, Ko En and Moung Pau-te, to seek out the members of the little church which was formerly in Ava. After a search of more than half a day, they found one individual, by the name of Ko Shway-nee,—and no language could express the feelings excited both ir him and his teacher at again meeting. "Amid all the trials and struggles," says Dr. Dawson, "to which he had been exposed, during the long period of seventeen years, his faith and hope as a Christian have remained unshaken. Many a bitter blast of temptation, of persecution and of worldly scorn has swept over his soul, and in the loneliness of his lot he supposed that God had forsaken him. But, casting away all fear, he has fought the good fight of faith and remained steadfast in Christ. When he heard that teacher Kincaid had arrived, his heart was filled with gladness, and down his furrowed cheeks flowed tears of joy! Of the old members of the Ava church, three of the venerable and aged had gone to their home in heaven. Others had left the city and settled elsewhere. A brother of Ko Shway-nee's wife had for a long period been an inquirer, and by gradually receiving instruction from his relative and looking to the Saviour for guidance, he finally settled down in the conviction that he was a Christian. His case was particularly interesting, inasmuch as it showed that God sometimes honors a very humble instrument to convert the heart of an unlettered Burman. This man proposes to accompany us down the river to Prome, where he wishes to be baptized. We rejoice in this first trophy of redeeming grace which has now become known to us, in the golden city of Ummerapoora."

At first considerable effort was made on the part

of a Jesuit priest and some of the officers to awaken prejudice in the king's mind against the missionaries, but all their devices signally failed, and in a few days they were sent for to go up to the palace. "To attempt any description of this magnificent establishment," says Dr. Dawson, "would require more time and space than I am now able to give it. It will suffice to say that it is built almost entirely of teak wood, lacquered, carved and gilded in a manner to make it an exceedingly imposing structure in the eyes of a stranger. Over the throne-room projects a spire, at once gorgeous and attractive. The height of it is probably about two hundred feet. The wings of the main building represent the figure of a cross. Next to it is the treasury, containing the crown-jewels; back of it is the garden; on one side is the royal tower, surmounted by a cupola; farther on is the royal stud, and at its side stands the palace of the 'white elephant.' Within the same enclosure are the arsenal and sheds for a great many guns. In front is a spacious building, constructed in the same style as the palace, known and occupied as the king's court. Here sit the woongees, or ministers of state, hearing and deciding cases, and administering laws which affect the entire kingdom. Surrounding the whole establishment are three walls, the outermost being a wooden palisade; the others are of brick.

Our first interview was with two of the At-wenwoons, or privy councillors, to whose private office we were led by Mr. Anthony Camarata, the collector of government customs. These functionaries received us with much friendliness, bade us sit down on the floor, and inquired into our business with the king. Mr. Kincaid mentioned that he lived in Ava during the reign of Noung-dau-pra, and left the capital soon after the accession to the throne of Thur-ra-wadi. We had now come simply to pay our respects to his Majesty, and to ascertain whether we might come up hereafter, and take up our abode near the 'golden feet.' Several other inquiries were then made of both of us, as to our particular professions, the kinds and cures of different diseases, surgical operations on tumors, on the limbs, and on the eyes; and other things pertaining to medicine. Appearing rather pleased, the two privy councillors rose, and, after adjusting their dress, said they would go up into the palace to see whether the king was at leisure, and requested us to remain for the present where we were. A crowd of people that thronged the office now broke away, and the officials passed out.

At half-past twelve, the collector called for us, remarking that the king was unengaged. Dropping our shoes at the bottom of the steps, we walked up, and were at once ushered into the royal presence.

His Majesty, the king of Burmah, was now before us!

His age is about forty-one ; his height is five feet seven inches. He is full and fleshy, without being fat, has a large, well developed head, particularly in the frontal region, and a noble brow. His countenance is pleasing, expressive of a thoughtful mind, cheerful temper and benevolent heart. He wore a rich silk 'patso' round his waist, but he had neither jacket nor head dress. His long black hair was rolled up into a knot at the top of his head. His features and complexion are of the ordinary Burman type.

Seating ourselves on the floor, as did everybody except His Majesty, and throwing our feet back into a most awkward and painful posture, with our hands upraised, we made our bow in the usual fashion observed at this court. The king nodded, as indicative of recognition. About thirty persons were in the chamber, who sat around in a semi-circle, and four sword-bearers, with their swords before them. The monarch was seated on a crimson velvet carpet, fringed with silk, and spread out on the elevated floor of the adjoining, but open apartment. A bolster reposed against one of the gilded posts of the room, against which the king reclined as he saw fit. We were formally introduced by the privy councillors as two American sayahs, (teachers,) one of whom (pointing to me) has some knowledge of medicine.

His Majesty opened the conversation by inquiring our object in coming to the capital. Fearing some impropriety in the expression of court terms and mode of address—words which are seldom or never pronounced in free America—we replied, mostly though not entirely, through Mr. Collector Camarata, that we had come up to present our respects to the king, and to get his authority to move up to the capital by-and-by with our families. He asked what we proposed doing? Our answer was, 'To instruct the people, to have a school for children, and to open a medical dispensary for the sick and suffering.' He then inquired how far America is from Burmah, how long it takes sailing vessels and steamers to make the passage out, the geographical situation of the continent of America, of Europe, and of various countries. He next spoke about the political relations existing between France and the United States, between France and England, and between England and America. Had England and America ever been at war? 'Yes, twice.' 'What was the result of those wars?' We replied, 'The American people got what they wanted. The first war obtained for them their independence; the second procured for them justice in regard to their commerce on the seas.' 'Have you a king in America, or what form of government have you there?' 'The government of the United States is a republic,—all the officers being elected by the people. The president, or chief magistrate, is elected every four years.' He shook his head, when told that the president is so frequently changed, and remarked that it was not a wise arrangement. He wished for information about the war now in progress with Russia, and the views entertained concerning it in the United States,—'because,' said he, 'not being mixed up in it, they would speak the truth.' He next asked, whether our coming up to his capital, and residing in it, would affect our political relations with our own government, or our right of citizenship in the United States. 'Not in the slightest,' we replied. He then inquired, 'Whether, if he wished us to go—one or both of us—to America upon his business, we would be willing to do so.' We answered that if his Majesty urged us to proceed to the United States on any important national business, for a short season, we could hardly refuse: that we would of course go ; but we hoped the king might have no reason for such a step.

He now repeated his question about the object of our visit to Ummerapoora, intimating somewhat pleasantly, that merchants, he knew, wished to acquire property and riches,—that scientific travelers passed through the country to observe its formation, and to notice curious and striking natural phenomena; there are others, whose design is not quite so clear, or creditable. By the latter class he evidently meant to say 'spies'—whose object is disreputable. This was the hardest remark that he made, and we could not fail to allow the credit of it to the wily Jesuit. We answered as before. 'But,' continued the king, 'Burmese children do not desire to study English.' We replied, that we never intended to teach them English; that there were a few foreigners' children who might wish to study it, but the Burmese ought to be taught knowledge; and there was a great deal of useful knowledge to learn. He then wanted to know when we would come up. We informed his Majesty that we could not leave our present stations at Prome and Rangoon, before other men from America should come to take our places. We hoped it would not be long, and that we should certainly, if Providence permitted, return again, at least to remain for a short period, during the next cold season. Turning to his officers on the opposite side, he observed, 'The white races are generally learned people; they are fond of books.'

The king now spoke about commerce, and said that he wished to encourage trade as much as possible. He requested us to write to the newspapers in America, and to inform our fellow-citizens, that he would do every thing in his power to promote trade. He hoped merchants would come and settle in his kingdom, that he would afford them every opportunity to obtain riches. We promised that we would make known his Majesty's sentiments. Mr. Kincaid offered to send him regularly the 'New York Weekly Tribune.' There are foreigners here who can translate it for him. 'He would be glad to see it, for,' said he, 'we can rely on it for particulars about the Russian war.'

His attention was next directed to a 'free-will offering' of books, which we had taken for the king's acceptance. He inquired what they were? We told him, calling out the names,—the 'Historical Instructor,' translated into Burmese by Mr. Stevens, for the government schools at Maulmain; a copy of Mr. Stilson's arithmetic in Burmese; a work by the same author on geometry, also in Burmese;—a little book on 'Human Anatomy,' translated by Mrs. Bennett,—and a richly bound copy of the Bible in Burmese. Speaking about books, he advised us to give no tracts or books to the Burmese; it would, he thought, be labor in vain. Some observations were now made respecting Burmese books, when the king remarked, that no man could read them all, they were so numerous, and not one in fifteen thousand could comprehend half of what he did read. His grand uncle, who was the most learned man in the empire, the celebrated Mekara prince, had read all the Burmese sacred books but one; though a most devoted student, he could not accomplish so great a task.

Our interview had now lasted nearly two hours, when his Majesty rose, and throwing his arms across his chest, and looking towards us, he said, 'If you have any feelings of regard for me,—in short, if you love me, *come soon, come soon*, and I will pay all your expenses.' He then turned, and retired into his private chamber.

Immediately the officers gathered round to look at the books; but they had scarcely opened them, when a lad came out and said, 'The king has sent for the books.' Before leaving the palace, we were informed that the king was engaged in reading them."

After remaining at the capital about a week, they returned to their homes at Prome and Rangoon, greatly encouraged with the prospect of reëstablishing the Ava mission, and rejoicing that the time had come when the gospel might be carried without hindrance to all the cities and towns of Burmah.

On the 24th of January, 1856, accompanied by their families, Messrs. Kincaid and Dawson again left Prome, on a second visit to the capital, where they arrived after a passage of twenty-five days. They were again received by the king in the most friendly manner, and strongly urged by him to take up their abode in the royal city. At their first interview with the king's brother he proposed committing to the care of Mr. Kincaid ten or a dozen young men, selected from some of the first families, to be taken to America for the purpose of acquiring an education in the higher branches of mechanical science; subsequently, however, it was thought best to abandon this scheme, and substitute a literary course at the "Doreton College," Calcutta.

But while that subject was engaging the thoughts of his royal highness, the king's mind was occupied with the project of despatching an official embassy to the government of the United States. For this service his Majesty was pleased to select Mr. Kincaid, engaging to pay all the expenses of the overland passage and back to Burmah. After some hesitation, Mr. Kincaid consented to the arrangement, and, a council of State having been held to consider the matter, a royal letter was at once prepared, and committed to the hands of Mr. Kincaid to be borne to the government at Washington.

In taking their leave of the court, Mr. Kincaid and Dr. Dawson were each presented with a silk patso, a ring, and a drinking cup, as marks of personal favor from his Majesty; while Mrs. Kincaid and Mrs. Dawson and the children were introduced to the queen and ladies at the palace, and were received with much cordiality. They gave a copy of the Burmese Bible to her Majesty, which was graciously and gladly accepted.

CHAPTER XXIII.

ON THE KING'S BUSINESS.

"I rose up and did the king's business."—Dan. viii. 27.

"Down the dark future, through long generations,
The sounds of war grow fainter, and then cease;
And like a bell with solemn, sweet vibrations,
I hear once more the voice of Christ say 'Peace.'
Peace! and no longer from its brazen portals,
The blast of war's great organ shakes the skies:
But beautiful as songs of the immortals,
The holy melodies of love arise."

HAVING consented to further the king's wishes with reference to the opening of friendly and commercial intercourse with the United States, Mr. Kincaid began at once to make his arrangements for another hasty visit to America. The opportunity of thus serving his Majesty was the more cheerfully embraced from the fact that the precarious state of Mrs. Kincaid's health seemed, again, imperatively to demand a change of climate. But for this consideration, his duty to the interests of the Mission would have been regarded as altogether too sacred to be neglected merely for the performance of a service not likely to result in any practical importance. Hoping, however, that a visit to his native land would restore his companion to her wonted health, he was induced to accept the king's appointment; and, accordingly, accompanied by his family, he left Rangoon, and was again on his way to America.

Shortly after his arrival here, he proceeded to Washington, and delivered into the hands of the President the Royal letter with which he had been intrusted, and of which the following is a literal translation. It was sealed with the king's seal, and inclosed in an elegant ivory box, lined with crimson velvet.

"His Majesty, whose glory is like the rising sun, ruling over the kingdoms of Tho-na-pa-yon-te, Yon-pa-de-pa, and all the eastern principalities, whose chiefs walk under golden umbrellas—Lord of Saddan, the King of Elephants, and Lord of many white Elephants—whose descent is from the royal race of Alompra,—also the great Lords and officers of State, ever bowing before his Majesty, as water lilies around the throne, to direct and superintend the affairs of the Empire—

Send salutations to the President and great officers of State residing in the city of Washington, and ruling over many great countries in the continent of America.

His Majesty, whose shadow, like that of his royal

race, falls over the entire kingdom, desires to govern so as to promote wise and useful regulations, such as the greatest of rulers has ever made it his study to accomplish. His Majesty is aware that it has always been the custom of great rulers to be on terms of friendship with other nations, and to pursue measures tending to perpetual amity.

As the American Teacher, Rev. E. Kincaid, has come to the royal city, without hindrance, and he has permission to go in and out of the Palace when he pleases, and has permission to look on the royal countenance, he will be able to address the President of the United States, and the great officers, on all subjects pertaining to the government and kingdom of Burmah. Should this royal kingdom and the great country of America form a friendly intercourse, there is on our part the desire that the two great countries through all coming generations may cultivate friendly relations—and that the merchants and common people and all classes may be greatly benefitted. For this purpose this royal letter is committed to Mr. Kincaid. Should he be chargod with a letter from the President and great officers of State, to bring to the royal city of Ava, for his Majesty and the court, and should the President and great officers say, Let the two countries be on terms of friendship, and that our children and grand-children, and all merchants and the common people, may through all generations reap great advantage—should such a message come, it will be heard with great pleasure."

To this letter the President prepared a respectful and appropriate reply, committing the same, with a large number of valuable national publications, to the care of Mr. Kincaid, to be delivered to the king.

The duties connected with this civil service were soon and easily accomplished. There were other matters, however, of an ecclesiastical character, which demanded his attention, and which were not so easily adjusted.

For a number of years serious difficulties had been known to exist between some of the Executive Committee, at Boston, and a large number of the Missionaries. These difficulties had now become so involved as to require a full and clear statement of all the facts in order that the integrity and honor of brethren in the foreign field might be vindicated. As one of their number—bound to each by strong fraternal ties, and familiar with all the points involved in the several cases—Mr. Kincaid came forward and stood nobly for their defence.

In his earnest vindication, as published,* will be found the principles for which Mr. Kincaid contended, as well as the motives which prompted him to

* This vindication appeared originally in the form of letters in the columns of *The American Baptist* and *Christian Chronicle.* These letters were subsequently issued in the form of a pamphlet.

take so conspicuous a part in this vexed and still unsettled controversy.

Let it here suffice to say, that the views sĕt forth in that vindication, were not reached in haste, nor were they advanced in a retaliative spirit of controversy. From the beginning of his missionary life he had boldly contended with all his prominent associates in labor, that the relationship subsisting between God's ambassadors who are sent to the foreign field, and the religious organization through which they derive their support, is not that of "*principal* and *agent*, *employers* and *employed*;" but strictly one of "*brotherly equality*," a relationship requiring them to look upon each other as *fellow-laborers* in the gospel. Hence, when the claim was officially put forth that "*the authority of the Board is absolute*," and when that authority, through the Executive Committee, issued instructions demanding "*acquiescence*"—under the claim of an "*absolute*" power—a power never conceded by the missionaries, and which they could not comply with except at the costly sacrifice of their individual responsibility,—Mr. Kincaid felt himself bound to protest against such usurped authority, claiming for himself and for his brethren the right of "*reciprocal direction*," and contending that no change should be made by either party without "*the consent of the other*."

In advocating this principle, Mr. Kincaid was led

to speak of particular instances in which he beleived it had been openly violated. Alluding for instance, to the case of Mr. Vinton, who was regarded as refractory, in having without authority removed from Maulmain to Rangoon, Mr. Kincaid, after fully explaining the circumstances which led to that important change, concludes by saying—" Did ' Mr. Vinton go to Rangoon on his own responsibility ?' One thousand Karen Christians called him to ' come over and help them.' Humanity with imploring voice called him ; above all, the Providence of God, in clear and distinct language, called him to the work. Dare he sit still, and say to these suffering Karens, and to weeping humanity, and above all to the Providence of God, ' Let me first go and obtain permission from those who claim dictatorial power over me ?' Dare he so insult the Providence of God, and mock the entreaties of God's suffering people ? Shall he say that he is a *hireling* and careth not for the torn and scattered flock ? Did ' Mr. Vinton go to Rangoon on his own responsibility ?' Shame, shame on such gross and fabulous statements. Never, since the day that Paul was called into Macedonia, has there been a clearer case of duty to go in the name of Christ. Had it been my case, under similar circumstances, no opposition on the part of man would have been regarded as of the slightest moment. I should have brushed them as cobwebs from my path. What power is that which thrusts itself between the ambassador of Christ in a heathen land, and the God of missions? What power is that which claims to keep the consciences of men who are planting churches on heathen shores?"

To the exercise of this power, claiming the right to give direction, but resisted by several devoted and successful missionaries, Mr. Kincaid ascribes all the difficulty which has for years disturbed our missionary operations. It is this, he contends, that has subjected them to the grave charge of "disregarding regulations" and "setting at naught instructions"; and impressed with the danger and evil consequent upon such an assumption of power, he says—"The cry of 'insubordination,' 'disregard of regulations,' 'setting at naught instructions,' is the cry of desperation.—Oppression has caused a revolt, not against regulations, but against outrage and wrong. Regulations are never *knowingly* disregarded. Oppression arouses, in self-defense, all but abject slaves." And then he adds—"Let any man or set of men be armed with dictatorial power, and there may be the exhibition of a *strong government*, to carry any measure, however unwise, to silence every murmur, however reasonable, and to crush all opposition, however just, as Louis Napoleon put France under his feet. Let every subject of importance be thoroughly ventilated and sifted. Let discussion, untrammeled by threats, be invited. Let all the aids of testimony, and the lights of experience and history be invoked. Let opinion grapple with opinion. This will be the most precious guaranty for the avoidance of evil, the security of sacred rights, and the preservation of truth. If infallibility is ascribed to one set of men, in such a sense as to require all their official acts to be sanctioned without examination, then a principle has been adopted abhorrent to Protestant Christianity."

The fearless avowal of sentiments like these had the effect, of course, to awaken, in some quarters, no little opposition, and not a few were disposed to regard their utterance in the light of a crime worthy to be treated as ecclesiastical treason. But neither fear nor favor could for a moment influence him to withhold the declaration of his honest convictions; and, with the same frankness and manliness which has marked his whole life, he has not hesitated to speak what he believed to be the truth, nor shunned the responsibility assumed in resisting what he has felt to be an encroachment on the Christian liberty of himself and his missionary brethren.

As on his two former visits to America, Mr. Kincaid's earnest addresses were everywhere listened to with the deepest interest, and his moving appeals in behalf of the perishing heathen never failed to meet with a cheerful and liberal response. But in addition to the service rendered to the general cause of missions, he was successful, through the voluntary contributions made at the close of his last public efforts in Philadelphia and New-York, in raising a fund of about a thousand dollars, which was judiciously expended in the purchase of a large assortment of educational works, and also of a number of astronomical instruments for the use of the Karen schools at Rangoon.

CHAPTER XXIV.

OVERLAND TO BURMAH.

"Behold, *the third* time I am ready to come unto you; and I will not be burdensome to you: for I seek not yours, but you."—2 Cor. xii. 14.

"O Burmah! shrouded in the pall
Of error's dreadful right!
For wings—for wings once more to bear
To thy dark shores the light."

On the second day of August, 1857, Mr. Kincaid, leaving his family behind him, again set out for Burmah. With the view of visiting Mrs. Kincaid's relatives in Scotland, he embarked for Glasgow, arriving there after a pleasant passage of fifteen days from New-York. Between four and five weeks were profitably spent in journeying through Scotland and England, and in both countries he received a most cordial welcome, and was frequently called upon to address very large assemblies on the subject of missions.

While in London, Mr. Kincaid embraced an opportunity of hearing the Rev. C. H. Spurgeon, at Surrey Garden, and the following extract from a letter, addressed to the Rev. N. Brown, D. D., will convey to the reader his impressions of that remarkable preacher, and, also, his views of church music—a topic at the present time exciting no little interest.

"The great edifice," he says, "with its three galleries, one above the other, and running round the entire building, was crowded to its utmost capacity. The sermon was plain, deeply practical, and delivered with an earnestness and pathos that held that vast assembly so still, that it seemed as if each one held in his breath. He drew such a picture of man's moral helplessness, and God's amazing grace and power to save, and pointed out so clearly man's utter ruin, and the revealed arm of Jehovah to save the penitent, that he certainly washed his hands of the blood of souls. The singing was almost overpowering. When that ocean of people rose and sung, 'Grace, 'tis a charming sound,' it seemed as if the windows of heaven were opened. This seemed like worshiping God, like making melody in the heart unto the Lord. How unlike this is an organ and a choir, making music for a sitting, silent congregation. To me it seems anti-christian. The noblest and most heavenly part of divine worship is handed over to a machine and a few hirelings. Why not hand over the praying to a few *hirelings?* It is time to amend our ways, and come back to the simplicity of the gospel."

Upon leaving England, Mr. Kincaid took what is known as the Overland, or Mail Route, to Calcutta, and some account of this passage, abounding as it does with information and incident, is here transferred from his journal:

Southampton, Oct. 20.—After breakfast I came on board the Indus. Every cabin is full, and at Malta we are to take on board two hundred or two hundred and fifty soldiers. We have passengers for Malta, Alexandria, Bombay, Ceylon, Madras, Calcutta, Burmah, Penang, and China. There are about thirty ladies, and all the rest officers and civilians. Lord Dalhousie with his two daughters are going to Malta to spend the winter. He recognized me as soon as I came on board, invited me to sit down, and we had a long conversation. He had learned long since that I had been to Ava, and that the king had been very cordial. Captain Maxwell, from Prome, is on board; he was engineer under Forlong. Several other officers have come up and called me by name. Some of them knew me in Rangoon, and others in Prome and Thayet.

Oct. 21.—Early this morning the mail steamer from Alexandria passed us. We have had a strong wind all day, with some rain; not more than half the passengers were at breakfast, and about the same at dinner. We are in the middle of the Bay of Biscay, and the sea is high.

Oct. 22.—Still in the Bay of Biscay. The weather is fine, but the sea is high. Only two ladies out at breakfast, and about half the gentlemen. There are four in my saloon, a room twelve feet square, and a table in the centre. Very comfortable. Then we have a small room adjoining, with a table and two couches. There are four rooms, with twenty passengers, all officers and surgeons but myself, and this saloon is for our exclusive use. The dining saloon above us is ninety feet long, and has two tables the entire length, and still there is not room for all the cabin passengers. We have tea or coffee at six in the morning, breakfast at nine, tiffin at twelve, dinner at four, and tea at eight. My health is excellent, and I am able to read and write all the time. Just now there is a heavy, rolling sea, and it is not very easy writing. By morning we shall be on the coast of Spain, and escape this heavy swell.

Oct. 23.—This morning at nine we were on the coast of Portugal. A lofty range of mountains are in full view. We do not stop at any port in Portugal. The wind is strong from the land, and is cold. There is but little sea, and the sun shines through a pale, hazy atmosphere.

Oct. 24.—This morning we are close in shore, about one mile distant, and are passing the mouth of the Tagus. About twenty miles up is Lisbon, the capital of Portugal. There is a fine, broad entrance, and beautiful high hills on each side. Four ships are just coming out to sea. One old castle is in sight, which was formerly used as a summer palace.

Lord's Day, Oct. 25.—This morning about ten, we were entering the Straits of Gibraltar. First we passed Cadiz, only two or three miles to the west, and soon the high coast of Africa rose gradually on the east. At eleven o'clock we had public worship, conducted by an Episcopalian clergyman. He did not attempt to preach, only read the service. At two o'clock we had the coast of Africa and of Europe close to us. Tangier is the largest sea-port of Morocco, the kingdom of the Moors, who once governed nearly all Spain. At half-past three we came to anchor in the bay of Gibraltar, about half a mile from the vast rock, which is supposed to be the strongest fortress in the world. The town is more than a mile long, and now in the evening, lighted up with gas, looks extremely well. The rock is so abrupt that the streets and houses can all be seen, one above the other. Vast excavations are made in the solid rock at different heights, where batteries of the largest sized guns are placed so as to sweep, with a whirlwind of balls, shot and shell, the whole bay and the low sand plain which connects it to the Spanish mainhead on the north-east side. The town has a population of seventy thousand, who are nearly all Spaniards and Maltese. On the Spanish side are three small towns in sight, built of stone, which look very pretty among the distant hills. A few miles below Gibraltar is the narrowest part of the straits, where Europe and Africa come within eight or nine miles of each other. We stop here six or seven hours to take in coal, and put off the mail.

Oct. 26.—This morning about eight, the snowy mountains of Sierra Nevada stood out in awful grandeur. They are said to be 12,000 feet high. The snowy ridges glisten in the sun beautifully. I should not think we were more than twenty miles distant from the coast of Spain. The coast of Africa is not in sight. Algiers is not far distant. This afternoon we are nearly opposite Carthagena.

Oct. 27.—On getting up this morning I found we were close to the African coast. Low ridges near the water, and then a succession of higher and still higher ridges back. Often we appear to be only two or three miles from the shore. Here and there smoke is curling up among the hills, and groups of cottages are seen, and now and then boats in the bays. A little after noon we pass the bay of Algiers, but so intercepted by hills that the city is now visible. The country along here for several hundred miles is now governed by France. Algiers is the capital, and a large sea-port. The country joins Morocco on the south. For many generations Algiers was the greatest place for pirates in the world, and thousands of

Europeans and Americans were captured, held in slavery, and made to work in irons. Popery and Mohammedanism have been the curse of this country. Before and after the Christian era, it was one of the most enlightened and prosperous countries in the world. A pure Christianity spread over all the coast of Africa, bordering upon the Mediterranean, but Popish dogmas gradually extinguished the light. Schools were declared to be a curse; ignorance, superstition and priest-craft following in rapid succession.

Ten o'clock, P. M.—We are now getting near the countries where Paul and his fellow-laborers toiled and suffered. What a burning shame that our missions in Greece, and France, and Africa, have been abandoned. Did we conduct missions in harmony with the spirit and genius of the gospel, the windows of heaven would be opened, and the churches at home would be like an army with banners. As it is now, we can expect little of the divine favor.

Oct. 28.—This morning we were still near the coast of Africa, and the sea for two days and nights has been as smooth as a pond. About sundown we were leaving the coast, and at ten in the evening we passed close under the island of Geta, two or three miles long, and having three or four islands much smaller near by. They are said to be of volcanic origin. The weather is becoming warm, and very fine; a gentle breeze from the African coast, but only a ripple on the water.

Oct. 29.—To-morrow morning early we expect to be at Malta, and there will be but little time for writing. I will dispatch this from that island, and write again from Alexandria. At times a feeling of sadness and gloom comes over me, but it does not last long. The promises of God are precious, and in every exigency he will be a present help.

Evening.—About three o'clock we passed close under an island called Pontenella. It is some thirteen or fourteen miles long, of considerable breadth, and is cultivated like a garden, almost entirely with grapes. It is the penal settlement of Naples. King Bomba sends all his state prisoners here. It is supposed the larger part of the convicts are among the best men of the State. A more cruel, brutal despotism does not exist probably in the world.

Malta, Oct. 30.—I have spent seven hours on shore. Viletta is the name of the town, built entirely of cream-colored sand-stone. The streets are extremely narrow, many of them not more than ten or twelve feet broad, and most of them are named after some saint, from the Roman calendar. The buildings are from three to four stories high; the population is about twenty thousand. The language is Arabic, somewhat modified and mixed up with Italian. There is a harbor on each side of the town, which is nearly surrounded by water, so that it is almost an island. It is a vast rock, rising many feet above the water, and above this rises a high wall of hewn stone, bristling in every direction with large guns. It is perhaps the strongest place in the world, after Gibraltar. St. John's church, built by the Knights of Malta, is the most remarkable edifice on the island. The roof is one vast arch of hewn stone, and entirely covered with paintings, intended to illustrate many events in Scripture history. The walls also are covered with similar paintings. The great altar in the centre transept is a masterly work; it is built of onyx and agate, topaz and lazuli. Behind the altar is a sculpture, as large as life, of Christ and John the Baptist, made from one piece of marble. John the Baptist is represented as pouring water from a large shell, on the head of Christ. There are several small chapels at right-angles with the main building, and all connected by a lofty arched way. All have their altars, sculptures, paintings, candlesticks and candles. All the candlesticks are of silver, and in the main building, before the high altar, they are about six feet high. The floor is made of sepulchral marble slabs, with various figures inlaid in mosaic work, in every variety of marble. It is the most remarkable building of the kind I have ever seen. It was built by the knights in the feudal ages, and is a monument of the darkness and superstition of those ages.

Alexandria, Nov. 2.—All last night we had on only half steam power, as we should reach the harbor before morning, but could not enter, as the channel is intricate. I was up by the earliest dawn. At first only a light from a lofty tower was seen, soon the faint outline of the coast became visible, next the palace buildings of the Pasha, on a point of land near the light-house tower. Soon the sun rose from the ocean and revealed the Nile, the city, the harbor crowded with ships, the forts bristling with guns, and several large men-of-war, and innumerable wind-mills along the coast as far as the eye could reach. In the distance Cleopatra's Needle, and a little farther inland Pompey's Pillar. After we entered the harbor we had a near view of many objects of interest. The anchor was no sooner down than large boats, filled with Egyptians and Abyssinians, came on each side of the ship, and began at once to carry off the baggage. Over these laborers were several grave, gentlemanly Turks and Arabs, neatly and even richly dressed. These men took an account of all the baggage of the passengers, and all the cases of military stores. After breakfast, the passengers took boats and went on shore, about one mile, and repaired at once to the office, and obtained tickets for transit through Egypt, across the desert to the Red Sea. About 11 A. M., the cars started, a very long train. The road for forty miles runs along the Viletta branch of the Nile. Here we crossed that branch, and what seemed to be a section of the bridge, worked by steam. Soon after crossing we entered a town of considerable size, where we had dinner, furnished by the Transit Company. After an hour we started off again, and every five or six miles passed through large villages or towns. The country is a dead level. Camels are seen in every direction; they are used for irrigating the land and also for carrying the produce to market.

Every town, and almost every village is surrounded by a wall made of bricks. All the buildings of the common people are made of sun-dried bricks, and only eight or ten feet square, many of them much smaller, and often made in the form of a bee-hive, with a small entrance. The land appears to be extremely fertile. The buffalo, such as we see in Burmah, is extensively employed in farming, but they are much smaller. Donkeys are used for riding, and even for carrying loads. Frequently I saw a camel and a buffalo yoked together ploughing. I saw vast fields of Indian corn, but it seems to be sown and not planted, and is small. The wheat harvest, and also that of peas and beans, is passed long since. Oranges, sweet limes, and pomegranates are in season. The pomegranates are three or four times larger than I ever saw in India, but the oranges are inferior. Cabbages and potatoes are abundant, but inferior in quality. Turks, Arabs, Greeks, and Armenians appear to be the great men, and to hold all the offices. The Egyptians and Copts are the laboring classes, and are in the lowest condition of servitude. There are also multitudes of Arabs and Abyssinians equally degraded. The distance between the high and low classes in Egypt is vastly greater than in Burmah, or even in Bengal. At 7 P. M. we entered Cairo, but many miles before reaching the city, we saw the far-famed pyramids, that is, the four within the neighborhood of Cairo. They are about four hundred feet high. From the sea-shore up to Cairo there are very few trees, except date trees, and these appear to be only twenty-five or thirty feet high.

Cairo, Nov. 3.—There are three hotels in the city, and they were nearly full when we arrived. The steamers from Calcutta, Bombay, and Australia, had come in to Suez, and all the passengers, or nearly all, had crossed the desert, and filled the hotels. Large numbers of us had to sleep on couches and benches —some on the floor ; and all the floors in Egypt are flag-stones, and rarely even covered with mats. About 9 P. M. we had supper, and then many of us took a walk through several streets. The atmosphere is wonderfully clear, and the moon rose beautifully, almost light enough to read any print. I slept on a couch without a pillow or a blanket, but my Scotch plaid did me good service, for it became cold before morning. Before sunrise scores of Arabs, with donkeys saddled, filled the whole space around the hotel. A very large number of the passengers took each a donkey and rode off to see the bazaars, the citadel, palace, and Pasha's Mosque. It was ludicrous enough to see the large, tall officers mounted on those little animals, not much larger than some of the goats I have seen in India. The fortress or citadel stands on a hill some two hundred feet above the town, and the view from its ramparts enables one to see the great desert on each side of the Nile. Except the narrow valley watered by the Nile and the canals, all is desolation, as far as the eye can reach. I went all over the mosque and the palace. They are built of Egyptian marble, unlike anything we ever see in America or England. The bazaars are much as we see them in Calcutta, only they are built of stone, and the second and third stairs jut out so that only a small opening is left for light to come into the narrow street below. At every step almost I met long lines of camels loaded with every conceivable article of use or of merchandize. Great numbers were loaded with building stone, and I should think each one carried five hundred pounds weight. They lie down like an elephant, to be loaded and unloaded, and I should think they were equally strong and docile as elephants. Carts and oxen are not used. I saw officials, Turks and Arabs, riding in English carriages with five horses and showy harness. There are a considerable number of costly buildings, but the great mass are low, dirty, miserable abodes. I saw one school of about forty boys. The only light and air came through the doorway ; the boys appeared to be from eight to fourteen years old. Old mats and gunny bags spread on the stone floor, made their seats. They all sat cross-legged on their mats, each one with a small coarse paper manuscript containing a few passages from the Koran. Simultaneously they all read in a peculiar sing-song tone, all as if by machinery heaved their bodies backwards and forwards, their heads nearly touching their books. Islanism appears to be all that is taught, and fanaticism of the worst character is fostered. The moral and intellectual condition of Egypt is as low perhaps as it can be. An iron despotism is everywhere visible. *Absolute power*, unmodified by any public opinion, has crushed out all sense of manliness ; beings made only a little lower than the angels are converted into mere animals, like beasts of burden. The curse of heaven rests upon this land.

Suez, Nov. 5.—I reached this place last evening about midnight, and am in the only hotel in town.—The waters of the Red Sea wash the stone steps on the eastern side. Back of the hotel lies the town, surrounded by a stone wall—one of the dirtiest and most miserable looking towns I ever saw. We left

Cairo yesterday about 11 o'clock, A. M., in the cars, and were soon in the Great Desert. The railroad is excellent, and is completed to within thirty miles of Suez. Nothing can exceed the utter desolation of the country, after leaving the Valley of the Nile.— No green thing is to be seen; there is no flower to 'waste its sweetness on the desert air.' The desert from the Nile to the Red Sea is not a dead level; the railroad is occasionally cut through elevations from five to ten feet, and in many cuttings I noticed a fine brown soil, and in several places layers of clay. This shows that only water is wanting to convert the desert into a rich, fertile country. True, some parts are only sand and pebbles. Occasionally I saw sand ridges many miles long, and thirty or forty feet high. These ridges all run east and west, and this shows that the strong prevailing winds are north and south, by the appearance of these sand-drifts. The strong and terrible winds which sometime sweep the desert are from the south, that is from Abyssinia. About forty miles from Cairo is a palace of the Pasha of Egypt, also several other buildings near it, and about two miles from the railroad. The Pasha with his court retires to this desert-palace when the plague is desolating the cities of the Nile. Every ten or fifteen miles is a building, and two or three scores of Arabs, with their small tents; these Arabs in case of any strong wind clear the sand-drifts from the rail. Here also is water in large iron tanks brought from the Nile, and coal to supply the locomotive. We saw several caravans of camels loaded, and moving on over the desert. They are truly called the ships of the desert; no other animal could live in such a desolate region. About 3 o'clock P. M., we came to the end of the railroad; here are three or four tents about sixty feet long and thirty broad, with tables and chairs to accommodate one hundred and fifty to sit down at their meals. Another tent to accommodate fifty or sixty second class passengers. There were in all about three hundred passengers. One freight train came in last night, and another will be in to-night. The scene at this place is novel and interesting. Some three thousand camels with their saddles on were lying or standing in groups, in every direction, ready to be loaded with baggage, mails and military stores. You may fancy the amount to be carried on camels from this to the Red Sea, about thirty miles, when these two hundred passengers have from three to six trunks each, and these trunks average one hundred pounds each. Then there are all the mails for Bombay, Ceylon, Madras, Calcutta, the Straits, and China. As the boxes lie on the plain they seem to be enough to load a three hundred ton vessel with the mails alone. Then there are fifteen hundred boxes of silver, nearly one million pounds sterling, for the army. It is said the silver alone will load a thousand camels. There are sixty thousand pairs of boots for soldiers, in fifteen thousand boxes, one thousand rifles in two hundred boxes, and besides all these, a vast amount of military stores. At half-past four, a hundred and eight passengers were sent off in eighteen vans, that is six passengers in each van. Each van is drawn by a pair of mules, and a pair of small horses. Two Arabs mounted on horses go along to keep the vans together. Every five miles the teams are changed, and at each place is a stone building, with a large court in the centre, where water, straw, and peas are kept for the animals. This water and provender is brought from the valley of the Nile. At half-past 8 P. M., one hundred and eight more passengers were sent off, and I was one of them. Till 10 o'clock it was very dark; then the moon rose and shed a beautiful, soft light over the desert. On our right, the whole distance to the sea, runs a broken range of hills, said to be from three to four hundred feet high, solid masses of rock. Our Arabs drove furiously, except in low places where sand had drifted. Occasionally for half a mile we seemed to be almost buried in the sand, and then again we would roll along on a smooth, hard surface, like a macadamized road. In several places we saw caravans of from one to two hundred camels. Each Bedowin has from four to seven or eight camels. He rides or leads one, and then the next, with a long cord, is tied to the saddle, and so on to the end, all following in single file. An Arab with eight or ten good camels will carry from four to five thousand pounds weight. All these inhabitants of the desert call themselves the children of Ishmael. For three hundred years they have been the same people, unchanged except by becoming the followers of Mohamet. During some four or five hours in the desert, waiting for the vans, I went around among these Ishmaelites, sitting in groups among their camels, to observe their features, the expression of the countenance, their conversation, and manners. I would have given anything to have been able to converse with them. I saw some noble features. Why is there not in all Christendom one or two men to consecrate themselves to the work of evangelizing this people? At first view it might seem hopeless, but I do not believe there is any insuperable obstacle in the way. Human wisdom would find difficulties enough and make mountains of mole-hills. In the promises of God there is no exception made; 'streams shall break forth in the desert, and springs in the dry and thirsty land.'

Ten miles before reaching Suez, we saw lights in the town and harbor, so level is the desert, and so clear is the atmosphere. It was midnight when we arrived, and one o'clock when we had supper, and then some thirty or more passengers had no bed.—During the night about two thousand camels loaded came in, and passengers continued to arrive until eight in the morning.

Nov. 7.—This is the third day we have been in this place, and we are to go on board the Hindustan this evening. The steamer for Bombay went off yesterday. The steamer for Australia that went off two weeks ago ran upon a coral reef, about eight hundred miles down the Red Sea, and stove a large hole in her bows. Being an iron ship, and having watertight compartments, only the part that was stove filled with water. After three or four days the tide rising, she got off, and has got back to Suez. What she will now do is uncertain. About thirty of her passengers, and also a hundred soldiers, will go with us, at least as far as Ceylon. So we have now in all seven hundred and twenty souls.

Nov. 8.—Just at dark last evening we steamed down the gulf of Suez ; both coasts are in sight all day, and often a very narrow channel, only seven or eight miles broad. About sundown we had a fine view of Mount Sinai, on the Arabian coast. On the other side was Nubia. When the wind blows from the African coast the heat is fearfully oppressive.—All is wild, desolate, and barren.

Nov. 13.—For three days we saw no land, except two or three vast rocks rising almost perpendicular from the sea. But yesterday and to-day we have passed great numbers of islands, and some of them very high. This afternoon we passed along within two or three miles of the Arabian coast, while the African coast is only a few miles distant. In the narrowest part of the channel is Perim, a small island where the English have sunk an Artesian well and found water ; their flag is now flying, and they are building a small fortress. It is admirably situated to command the entrance to the Red Sea. It is only some seventy miles above Aden, where we expect to be to-night."

Without following Mr. Kincaid in all the subsequent details of his journal, it may suffice to say, that upon reaching Aden, one day was required to take in coal. This afforded a very favorable opportunity of seeing the town. It contains a population of 20,000, and is not particularly interesting, being chiefly remarkable for its barren, bluish-colored hills. The houses are built of bamboo, and on a foundation of sand. Four miles in the interior is the Turkish wall, where the British military force is situated. The next stopping place in the voyage was at Ceylon. Here, also, a day was very pleasantly spent. This island is not only a bustling, business-like place, but one of extraordinary beauty, and hence, styled by the natives a "terrestrial paradise." It is situated in the Indian Ocean, near Cape Cormorin ; is 270 miles long, 150 broad, and has a population of 1,130,000 souls. In the interior there are several cities and towns, one of which (Candy) contains a public library, erected on pillars, and built in a lake.

Off the northwest of Ceylon is a great and valuable pearl fishery. The natives are of Hindoo origin, and under British rule, are fast advancing in cultivation and wealth.

Once more on the deep, and four days brought them before Madras. This is the capital of the presidency of that name, and is situated in the Carnatic, on the shores of the Bay of Bengal. So low is the shore here, that a landing can only be effected in native barges, called massoollah boats. These are well manned, however, and so skillfully handled that they dash with safety through the heaviest surf. The population of the city is between four and five hundred thousand.

Three days more on ship board, and they enter the mouth of the river Hooghly, and after steaming 100 miles, they drop anchor before Calcutta—the city of palaces, and the capital of British India. It is upwards of six miles in length, extending along the river's bank. The population is about 600,000, and, like the other principal cities under British rule, of a very mixed character, affording the stranger no small amount of amusement in the way of costume and physiognomy. Many of the houses are tall and stately, with verandas and Grecian pillars. Behind the front lines of mansions is the native town, with dirty, narrow streets, dirty natives—all more or less naked—ghastly religious mendicants, showy marriage processions, and sounds of creaking wheels and discordant voices. From the quay, built by Lord Hastings, we may see all this, and also the vessels of every shape and size from all parts of the world; while near the banks are hundreds of Brahmins, saying their prayers and washing in the deified river.

Mr. Kincaid landed in Calcutta late on Saturday evening, the 5th of December. He says in a letter, dated Dec. 8, "It was just three months from the day I left New York to the day I landed in Calcutta, and I spent thirty-three days in England, five days in Egypt, one day in Aden, one in Ceylon, besides stopping a few hours at Gibraltar, Malta and Madras, so that I made the voyage in little less than fifty days."

After spending two weeks in Calcutta, during which time several interviews were had with Dr. Duff and other missionaries, Mr. Kincaid again embarked, arriving in Rangoon toward the close of December. In a letter from him, bearing date of January first, he states that he was then about starting for Prome, intending, after visiting the churches there, to proceed up to Ava. He had just learned that his Majesty had been anxiously inquiring when he was to return, and that a rumor had reached Rangoon that the king had turned all the priests out of the city, and that he was constantly reading Jesus Christ's book.

CHAPTER XXV.

RETROSPECT AND PROSPECT.

"He hath showed his people the power of his works, that he may give them the heritage of the heathen."—Ps. cxi. 6.

> "Are there not signs,
> Thunders and voices, in the troubled air?
> Do ye not see, upon the mountain tops,
> Beacon to beacon answering? Who can tell
> But all the harsh and dissonant sounds which long
> Have been—are still—disquieting the earth,
> Are but the tuning of the varying parts
> For the grand chorus, which shall usher in
> The hastening triumph of the Prince of Peace!
> Yes; his shall be the kingdoms.
> * * * * * *
> E'en now the symphonies
> Of that blest song are floating through the air—
> Peace, peace on earth, and glory be to God."

In looking back over the period of Mr. Kincaid's labors, how changed is the moral aspect of the people among whom he has gone preaching the gospel!—When he entered the field, Burmah had, as it were, but just heard the name of Christ, and the number of conversions from heathenism was comparatively small. For several years, amid many privations and bitter persecutions, the first devoted band of Missionaries had sought to prepare the way and to lift up a standard for the people. At that time the measure of missionary spirit in the churches was very limited, and many felt but little confidence in the success of the efforts that were making for the salvation of the heathen. "They had but little to rest on," said one of their number, "except the command and promise of God." The faith of many faltered. The work advanced but slowly, and so numerous were the impediments thrown in the way, both at home and abroad, as almost to forbode defeat. Dr. Morse, in his Universal Gazetteer, published about this time, said, under the head of Rangoon—"The American Baptists have employed two missionaries here; but, owing to the opposition of the Burman government, it is supposed they will be obliged to leave the country."

Amid all the trials and discouragements, however, which beset those who were *first* in the field, their faith did not fail them, and they were enabled to prosecute their work with a joyful and unwavering confidence of ultimate success.

Now, how changed is the aspect of things! The government that then sought to banish Christ's ambassadors, desires to foster them; and, in the exercise of his royal favor, the king extends to them the freedom of the empire!

At home, too, public sentiment respecting Foreign Missions has undergone a radical change; and the enterprise has now come to be regarded as one of the noblest that can possibly enlist the sympathies and efforts of the Christian church.

The influence of this work at home, as well as its results abroad, are beyond all human computation.—That our churches have felt a powerful reflex influence from the foreign field, cannot be doubted, and it would not be difficult to show that the activity and resources of the church owe their development more to this enterprise than to all other agencies combined. But within the last thirty years what an immense amount of good has been accomplished on the field, while, at the same time, deep and strong foundations have been laid for the achievement of still larger results. The entire Bible has been translated into the language of the people—books have been prepared—schools established—churches organized—the Gospel has been preached in almost every part of the empire, and thousands of souls have there been brought to a saving knowledge of the Lord Jesus Christ. With these facts before him, and in the exercise of strong faith in God, Mr. Kincaid might well write—"The mission in Burmah cannot be overthrown; it is founded upon the Rock of Ages; the gates of hell cannot prevail against it; the prayers of God's people have been heard. The gospel of Christ in its blessed revelations has been preached in thousands of Burman cities and villages, from the sea-shore up to the lower Himalayas, and in thousands of Karen hamlets. God's holy word is read not only by thousands of Karens and Burmans of the common people, but in the palace of Alompra. There is not only a shaking among the dry bones, but the Holy Spirit has been poured out, and a great army is standing up on the side of the Lord of Hosts. There are ministers of Christ standing on those out-posts of Zion's walls, and leading forth those converts into the thickest of the war, and teaching them how to work for God. No dangers can alarm them, no opposition can discourage them, and no persecution can crush them. He who said, 'Be not afraid;' 'Lo, I am with you;' stands at their right hand and girds them with strength."

But cheering as have already been the triumphs of the Gospel in Burmah, the day, we are persuaded, is not distant that shall witness still greater conquests; and, though before that day dawn, the present race of devoted laborers may be in their graves, their successors will certainly see it, and, going forth with a sublime faith in the Divine promises, and with hearts full of love and zeal for the Divine glory, it shall be their great joy to witness the gathering of all the people unto Shiloh.

Nor will this success be limited to Burmah. The enterprise of Christian Missions contemplates not the subjugation of a nation, but the conquest of the world ; and, looking into the future, we are permitted to see cheering evidence that the victories of the cross are fast hastening to a glorious consummation. Said Dr. Judson, in his farewell address—

"Judging from the past, what may we rationally expect during the lapse of another thirty or forty years? Look forward with the eye of faith. See the missionary spirit universally diffused, and in active operation throughout this country,—every church sustaining, not only its own minister, but, through some general organization, its own missionary in a foreign land. See the Bible faithfully translated into all languages,—the rays of the lamp of heaven transmitted through every medium, and illuminating all lands. See the Sabbath spreading its holy calm over the face of the earth,—the churches of Zion assembling, and the praises of Jesus resounding from shore to shore,—and, though the great majority may still remain, as now in this Christian country, without hope and without God in the world, yet the barriers in the way of the descent and operations of the Holy Spirit removed, revivals of religion shall then become more constant and more powerful. The world is yet in its infancy: the gracious designs of God are yet hardly developed. Glorious things are spoken of Zion, the city of our God. She is yet to triumph, and become the joy and glory of the whole earth.—Blessed be God, that we live in these latter times,—the latter times of the reign of darkness and imposture. Great is our privilege, precious our opportunity, to coöperate with the Saviour in the blessed work of enlarging and establishing his kingdom throughout the world."

The promises of God are all pledged to his Son for a universal triumph—the field of labor assigned to the church covers the entire world, and the prayer that is constantly ascending to heaven from the heart of every true believer is, that the heathen may be given to Christ for an inheritance, and the uttermost parts of the earth for a possession. And when this prayer shall be answered—when this field shall be cultivated—when this pledge shall be redeemed—then " He shall have dominion from sea to sea, and from the river unto the ends of the earth"—" The mouth of the Lord hath spoken it." And—

" May the hour
Soon come, when, all false gods, false creeds, false prophets,
Demolished, the round world shall be at last
The mercy-seat of God, the heritage
Of Christ, and the possession of the Spirit!"

A

CATALOGUE

OF

POPULAR BOOKS,

SOLD BY

TRAVELING AGENTS.

NEW-YORK:

H. DAYTON, PUBLISHER,

107 NASSAU-STREET.

WESTERN BRANCH—DAYTON & ASHER: INDIANAPOLIS, IND.

J. J. Reed, Printer & Stereotyper, 16 Spruce-St., N. Y.

42,000 SOLD, AND THE DEMAND CONSTANTLY INCREASING.

THE

PRINCE OF THE HOUSE OF DAVID;

OR,

THREE YEARS IN JERUSALEM,

IN THE DAYS OF PONTIUS PILATE.

The book is a large 12mo. vol., of 500 pages, and is embellished with a steel plate Portrait of the

BEAUTIFUL JEWISH MAIDEN,

An Engraved Title Page, and seven large, splendid Engravings, from entire new designs, and executed by the first artists in the country, making altogether one of the most beautiful and interesting books ever offered to the American public.

The Author and Publishers being anxious to place the book in the hands of every person that is able to read, have fixed the price at

THE LOW SUM OF $1 25.

———o———

From the Christian Advocate and Journal.

This is certainly among the most delightful volumes we have ever read. It is very ably and most eloquently written. No novel or romance could be more efficient in its effect on the imagination or the affections of the heart; while its facts and incidents are in keeping with the evangelical records. It is a book which one would read again and again, for the delightful and sanctifying emotions it awakens in one who feels and realizes his personal interest in the " story of the cross."

From the Dispatch, Richmond, Va.

Jesus was *man*, as well as God! In this book He is seen, conversed with, eaten with as a man! The book presents him in the social and moral relations of life, with exemplary fidelity to the Scripture narrative, and yet with a freshness which falls upon the mind like a new and thrilling narrative, and a life-likeness in every lineament which we feel must be true to the original. In truth, the reader, no matter how conversant with the sacred writings, is drawn along with breathless interest, and the very depths of his heart reached and stirred into uncontrollable emotion. Outside of the Holy Gospels themselves, we have never seen so moving a picture of the life of the Man of Sorrow, nor any representation of the wondrous b[illegible], of the Divine character, so touching and so true.

THE PRINCE OF THE HOUSE OF DAVID

WILL BE SENT BY MAIL, POSTAGE PAID, TO ANY PART OF THE UNITED STATES, OF RECEIPT OF THE PRICE, $1 25.

AGENTS WANTED in all parts of the country to engage in its sale.

Address, **H. Dayton,** Publisher,

No. 107 NASSAU-ST., N. Y.

www.ingramcontent.com/pod-product-compliance
Lightning Source LLC
LaVergne TN
LVHW020222110826
845151LV00003B/801

* 9 7 8 1 4 2 5 5 3 2 9 1 8 *